JUST MEN

GORDON RUPP

JUST MEN

Historical Pieces

LONDON
EPWORTH PRESS

Enquiries should be addressed to
The Methodist Publishing House
Wellington Road
Wimbledon
London SW19 8EU

7162 0267 0

Printed in Great Britain by
The Garden City Press Limited
Letchworth, Hertfordshire SG6 1JS

For
W. GARFIELD LICKES

Contents

Preface

The historical sketches here assembled were occasional pieces. prompted by various invitations on very diverse occasions. But there will be apparent, I hope, an underlying unity. That a Methodist should be invited by Anglicans to speak about Matthew Parker, by the Church of Scotland about John Knox, and by Catholics about Newman, is proof of the splendid gestures of our ecumenical age – unthinkable half a century ago, and worth remembering in a decade half-ashamed of its generosities. It is also, I should like to think, a witness of a Catholicity defined by John Scott Lidgett when he wrote. 'Not a saint, not a thinker, a hero or a martyr of the Church, but we claim a share in his character, influence and achievements, by confessing the debt we owe to the great tradition which he has enriched by saintly consecration, true thought or noble conduct.' I own to some little mental fight about one or two of those invitations; and to some hard thinking and reading before I could confess the degree of sympathy with the subject which would be proper to a celebration, for I have no liking for those who go out of their way to vent their spleen on the illustrious dead. 'Just Men' is perhaps a pun, or a double-edged word. This little band of Christian men shared a common integrity and, more than they knew, a common faith. And it might be hoped that these essays would enable us to understand why Holy Writ bids us mark such men. The phrase also reminds us that they were mortal men, rooted in their age. And the poignant comment of Matthew Parker, in the margin of Sir John Cheke's pathetic recantation, 'Homines sumus' ('we are, after all, only men') – close as it is to Martin Luther's famous last written words : 'Poor beggars are we all' – would have seemed to all these worthies a true comment on themselves.

Epiphany, 1977   GORDON RUPP

1

Benedict, Patron of Europe*

As a methodist and a Protestant I am both honoured
and abashed to be in this place with this theme. When I discovered that my lecture was to fall between two discourses by
distinguished sons of Saint Benedict's own Order, and when I
talked about it, on the steps of the British Museum last week, to
one of them, David Knowles, a consummate historian who has
devoted his life to this very theme, I was in near-despair and I
turned for comfort to the Rule of Saint Benedict, Chapter 68. 'If
a brother be commanded to do impossible things . . .'. I found
it written :

> he sees that the weight of the burden altogether exceeds the
> measure of his strength . . . let the subject know that it is
> expedient for him.[1]

Perhaps there is one point in my appearing here. In this decade
of Vatican II, we are all learning to think not only of our own
things but also of the things of others. A few weeks ago, Monsig-
nor Cardinale delighted the World Methodist Council in London
by describing Duns Scotus, a little exuberantly, as the first
Methodist. It almost encourages me to talk about John Wesley
as the last Benedictine, or at least to say that the Rule of Saint
Benedict is a right Methodist epistle. But above all what matters
is neither Protestant nor Catholic, but what is mere Christian –
the urgent and difficult problems confronting all the Churches in
mission and communication to the present age. No doubt the
differences between our world and that of Saint Benedict are
more obvious than the similarities, but when David Knowles says
that the sixth century was a new adolescent age of shifting
landmarks, this rings a bell. For there is nothing more ironical

---

* An Address given in Coventry Cathedral during the Symposium, 'A
Vision of Europe', July 1967

than the way in which we speak nowadays of mankind coming of age, and of mature Christianity, when all the facts point to this as being an age of adolescence, where, in mind and spirit, leadership has passed to two great overgrown schoolboy nations, America and Soviet Russia. For adolescence, as the late Professor Victor Murray once said, does not mean what happens to young people between fourteen and twenty-two, so much as a sense of being surrounded with problems which we cannot cope with out of our inner intellectual and emotional resources; a world of instability and moods and uncertainty. But by calling adolescence the mark of our society, I do not intend disparagement of the youth of our day. With due deference to the distinguished speaker here this evening, I find more of the authentic spirit of Saint Benedict in young people sitting down on pavements in Downing Street and Whitehall, in Westminster, than those who sit up inside behind their desks. It was after all what happened to Benedict as a teenager which changed history.

We meet him as that rather unfashionable figure today, a privileged son of the establishment. Son of a Roman patrician, as might be a modern sixth-former, a prefect from Harrow or Winchester, on the run from school, accompanied by, above all things, his Nannie. And when he tore himself away from her apron strings, it was to plunge with all the gusto and extravagance of youth into the wildest of all adventures, the search for God. And perhaps this is why Benedict inserts in his Rule a phrase which would still shock many trustees of church youth clubs and Senates of not a few universities: 'God often reveals what is best to the younger one.' And when we consider the three Benedictine vows, stability, or as we might say today, stickability, conversion of manners and obedience, are not these tailored exactly to adolescent needs? And, dare we add, since the young today appear to be able to work only when surrounded by loud and preferably stunning noise, the medicine of silence and of quiet? And a world without landmarks. The unity, always precarious, of the Roman Empire, that Hellenist and Roman culture, had split apart, and while in the east the Byzantines tried desperately, and in the age of Justinian not unsuccessfully, to hold a slippery greatness, the western half had dissolved under the stress of war and invasion from Byzantine armies and barbarian tribes.

None knew this better than Roman patricians, though for most of them the signs were humdrum practical things which C. S. Lewis once listed as 'worse houses, worse drains, fewer baths, worse roads and less security'. And when Benedict stopped running, it was to hole up in a cave with a view of the ruins of Nero's palace by the long reeds of a lake and the broken arches of a Roman aqueduct. This is the grim and desolate stage across which intermittently barbarian chiefs like Totila the Goth stride like strange visitors from another planet, demanding, 'Take me to your leader'. Across the west, in Italy and Gaul and Spain, Christian Churches were left isolated like half-eroded sand castles amid the scum of each incoming and destructive wave. Christian men looked back nostalgically over little more than a century to the brave beginnings of the Christian empire, to the age of the Fathers, much as we look back to the eminent Victorians, with Athanasius and Augustine, Basil and Jerome, for Darwin and Livingstone, Lincoln and Tennyson, and its noble Christian women, its Monnicas and Macrinas, for the Brontës and Miss Nightingale. And they remembered the brilliance of Basil and Jerome, while the splendid panorama of Augustine's *City of God*, the hall-mark of which is that peace which is the tranquillity of order, seems to mock a new world in all things its antithesis. If we had to find a text for Benedict, might it not be 'In the days of Noah while the Ark was a preparing'? The older monks, Antony and Pachomius, Macarius and Cassian, had founded communities and devised rules, but could such frail craft survive the rising storm? To build an ark not made with hands into which, two by two, human and eternal values might enter, to be kept until the waters assuaged and then to be brought safely out into a new world, this was the achievement of Saint Benedict and that ark was his Rule. So he left the world to find God. He explored alone, as Sir Francis Chichester the ocean, and Gagarin outer space. To many today this is the wrong way of doing it. Our magic word is 'involvement'. But in fact there has to be in Christian history a double rhythm of involvement and disengagement. When the first Christians publicly repudiated the pomps of the world, the flesh and the devil, it was not just escapism; it was not just a platonic or gnostic disparagement of earthly goods, of the body, of the things of time and sense. When near the end of his life Benedict saw in a vision the whole world caught in a

3

sunbeam, and said, '*inspexi et despexi*' ('I saw it and I disdained it') it was a repudiation of the world in the sense in which his Master had also refused its glories when he saw them from the pinnacle of the temple in Jerusalem. The primary call to the Christian is to deny himself and take up his cross, to lose his life if he would save it, and to seek first and at all costs the kingdom of God and his righteousness. If we forget these priorities, then involvement becomes a dangerous two-way traffic in which the Church may easily be submerged and become adjectival to another way of life, Roman, Gothic, American or European. We see the marks of this in the sixth century, in the infiltration through the Goths of the Aryan heresy and in a more subtle infection of ideas about God and man which, as Jungmann has shown, left their effects upon the Church's sacraments and liturgy. Gregory the Great at this point comments, in the story of Benedict, that 'a man may lose hold of his own soul yet fail to find those of his fellows'. And perhaps this kind of ineffectual half-way house is where the modern Church is heading through its pardonable obsession with communication. But this is the three-fold call : disengagement, commitment, involvement. This is how a solitary man at his prayers could become patron of Europe. It is not only the Benedictine, it is the ultimate Christian paradox.

In our world of steel and concrete we may forget that a man praying is a scientific marvel, as mysterious and intricate as the radio telescope at Jodrell Bank. And both are places where men listen for signals from 'out there'.

> Let us open our eyes to the divine light [said Benedict] and let us hear with attentive ears the warning that the divine voice crieth daily to us : and when you have done these things my eyes will be upon you and my ears open unto your prayers. And before you call upon me I shall say to you, Lo! here I am.

A God who is out there, a God who is not in us but beyond us! This may shock our current immanentism, but I suggest that if you study the recently published essays from the first round of the continental Marxist/Christian dialogue, you will find much support for the view that it is precisely what Christianity has to say about a God who lies without nature and beyond history which is the one thing that the Marxist cannot understand, and yet most needs to know. And so in contrast to the current kitchen-sink school of prayer, of which we have so much just now, the spate of pseudo-Quoist which bids fair to be as depressing in this decade as pseudo-T. S. Eliot was in the last, Saint Benedict insists firmly that there shall be a place where nothing is put and nothing done but prayer. One of Gregory's stories is of a monk who stopped saying his prayers for very much the same reasons as Bishop J. A. T. Robinson describes what happened to him in college : 'For he could not continue at his prayers, for when other monks kneel to serve God, his manner was to go forth and with a wandering mind to busy himself about earthly things.' I know young clergymen who have stopped saying their prayers in favour of being involved with people. Well, what they consider a virtue, Benedict thought to be a rather subtle temptation. And we are told that he waited on this restless and rather arrogant young man (the Winchester and Harrow prefect touch again!) with a cane and one of the best. But Benedict went away not only to be alone with God but to learn to live with himself : to listen to the voices of that soul which, as Turgenev said, is as full of murmurs as a dark forest. He looked not only up to God whose glory is beyond the light of setting suns, but down into his own heart, into that conscience which Augustine says is an unsearchable abyss. Not just to stare placidly as a man might find his face mirrored in the waters of a lake, but like wrestling Jacob, in sweat and agony, in that grim fight for which Luther gave the special name *Anfechtung*.

But Benedict's Noah's ark – or if you prefer it, his Christian space station – contained a family.

At the heart of the Christian religion is the beloved community, the *koinonia*, the Christian group or cell; and the secret of true community is not in the casual brushing shoulders of the streets of the secular city, or of dwellers in flats or seaside hotels. The Benedictine Rule is for a common life, because Christianity is a team game, because its virtues cannot be exercised in a vacuum or grown in isolation but need a Christian family small enough for its members to know one another very well indeed, to watch over one another, to bear with one another's weaknesses and rejoice in one another's victories. God and conscience and the communion of saints : these are the priorities of disengagement. But no less important is commitment.

> Faithfully fulfil the instructions of a loving father [says Benedict] that by the labour of obedience thou mayest return to him from whom thou hast strayed by the sloth of disobedience. Fight for the true King, Christ, [and] take up the strong and glorious weapons of obedience.

I think Saint Gregory's Life of Benedict leaves him still very much a faceless man. These stories about the old desert fathers and the monks are a little like the stories of Oxford and Cambridge eccentric dons in the last century. We can be fairly sure, for example, that Dr Spooner spoke spoonerisms, without having to be committed to any one anecdote. And I find myself rather a falling off in credibility between the life of Saint Antony by Athanasius the century before and these thaumaturgic anecdotes of Saint Gregory. So many of the miracles of Benedict, if I may use a rather risky discrimination, seem to be Old Testament rather than New, Elijah- and Elisha-like, as though we had a collection of jokes where the point of each story has been turned into a platitude. It is a wonderful and refreshing contrast to turn from these things to the Rule itself; for it is the Rule of Benedict which gives him his face, which bears the mark of a personality, which is as striking and recognizable as a fugue by John Sebastian Bach or a picture by El Greco. And for all its debt to others, as a patchwork of quotations from Holy Scripture and holy men and holy rules, it has its own authentic character as a classic. So that I think that nobody who has to live in any kind of Christian community could read it without profit for its charitable and kindly and always practicable wisdom. Dorothy Sayers once wrote about the lost tools of learning, but here are other lost tools, the tools of virtue and of goodness : a Rule which expounds a pattern of character in which Hellenic and Roman and Christian ideals blend, whose moderation made it possible for the monastic life to flourish in the western world and be adapted to colder and northern climes. As in private duty bound I may say that no historian has spoken more appreciatively of this than a Methodist Church historian, H. B. Workman, who singles out its appeal to consience and its great emphasis on self-surrender rather than on self-conquest. It is very interesting to turn, as I did the other day, from reading the Rule of Saint Benedict to what I suppose is its most powerful modern rival, the sayings of Mao Tse-tung, and see the contrast of the brutal platitudes of a rigid legalism and authoritarianism, of which sometimes monasticism has been accused. But the Rule of Saint Benedict is not a Christian Torah; if it is a highway code it is set to music, its statutes have become songs.

> As we progress . . . our hearts shall be enlarged [says Benedict] and we shall run with unspeakable sweetness of love in the way of God's commandments.

And yet for all its inwardness, it is a way by which men can walk, the terms of reference in a partnership of work and prayer, the heart of which is worship and *lectio divina* in the Bible and the Psalms. I sometimes think the one thing that Methodists might do for a united Anglican/Methodist Church is to give back the Psalms to Anglicans, who have got tired of them. In this week's *Times Literary Supplement*, a writer disparages a recent book on poetry and prayer, and concludes, 'But what has prayer to do with poetry?' The answer is: 'Read your Psalms.' The Psalms remind us that the language at the heart of the Christian tradition has more about it of poetry than prose. More indeed of the imbalance and extravagance of a love letter than the formal precision of a notice board. Prayer – and with it hard work. I like the story of Benedict's Goth who could not read but could work, and who laid about him at the reeds and rushes with such passion that the bill flew from off its hook and vanished in the waters of the lake, only to get a severe rebuke from brother Maurus who seems to me to have been a shop steward of the baser sort.

From disengagement and commitment comes involvement. And this is how Newman put it in a classic statement:

> The new work which Benedict helped to create was a growth rather than a structure. Silent men were observed about the country, were discovered in the forest, digging, clearing and building, and other silent men, not seen, were sitting in the cold

cloister, tiring their eyes and keeping their attention on the stretch while they painfully copied and re-copied the manuscripts which they had saved. And by degrees the woody swamp became a hermitage, a religious house, a farm, an abbey, a village, a seminary, a school of learning, a city.

Or more precisely in the words of J. S. Brewer:

If men know how to farm and drain and till the land scientifically, if they know how colleges may be built and large households maintained without confusion, if they have learned to value economy, punctuality and despatch, nay more, if the minor obligations of social life, the unwritten laws of natural respect, good breeding and politeness, have grown among men, these were all derived from the monasteries, for their discipline reached from the highest to the lowliest duties of men, as if all were bound together in one indissoluble union.

And as a succession of stones thrown into a pond will raise widening ripples which intersect until at last the whole surface of the water is agitated, so there went out from the scores of monasteries an ever-extending influence. What is meant on the grand scale you can read about in such books as Christopher Dawson's famous essay, *The Making of Europe*. Benedict himself, I suppose, would hardly have understood the word 'Europe'. For him the three parts of the habitable world had been divided once for all among the sons of Noah, Shem, Ham and Japheth; and Italy and what lay around it and beyond it to north and west lay within the patrimony of Japheth; and, rather importantly, between Benedict and Europe there intervened another great entity, that of Christendom. Benedict is not only a patron of Christendom, but almost *patron* in the Maigret sense, the boss who stands smiling in the background, washing the glasses in the Maigret plays. There was first of all the missionary apostolate to the barbarians and, in the wake of evangelism, new patterns of manners and behaviour almost startlingly swift in influence. As I have seen in Fiji, the grandchildren of converted cannibals in neat school uniforms, reading *Barchester Towers* for a Cambridge Certificate, so in the seventh and eighth centuries there are the schools of Alfred and of Alcuin and the astonishing court of Charlemagne; and in the monasteries, learning and libraries, the glories of Monte Cassino, St Gall, Bobbio, the renewals of monasticism itself, Cluny and the Cistercians and the Charter-house; and – because, as we said, involvement is always a two-way traffic – a rather dangerous involvement with the corridors of political power along which Pope Gregory VII so purpose-fully trod, and with it too involvement in the fabric of law and social life. And as the monasteries amassed great possessions and their leaders became feudal dignitaries, giving temporal service and political counsel to kings and princes, they were the pillars of the emerging unity of culture, that Christendom whose unity was broken from within only by Jews and heretics and threatened from without by the Saracens. Of this culture the flowering in the twelfth and thirteenth centuries were the cathedrals and the universities, the cities and the coming of the friars. The earliest and I suppose the most authentic portrait of Saint Francis is that to be found at Subiaco, which he visited to draw constantly upon the inspiration of Saint Benedict to transmute it into his own idiom, and of this culture the fruits that followed the flowers were the new energies of the emerging nations, the birth of what we can now recognizably speak of as Europe. Professor Denys Hay of Edinburgh has written an illuminating and very learned study of this use of the word 'Europe' and the conception of it in history. And he suggests that we find it earliest and most clearly stated at the beginning of the humanist renaissance in the writ-ings of Pope Pius II, who in a letter to Mahomet II, the con-queror of Constantinople, speaks about 'Christendom', in the new European term.

> We cannot believe that you are unaware of the resources of the Christian people, how strong is Spain, how warlike France, how numerous are the people of Germany, how powerful Britain, how bold Poland, how vigorous Hungary, how rich, spirited and skilled in warfare is Italy.[2]

An impressive catalogue, though hardly of the Benedictine virtues.

At the beginning of the seventeenth century, Samuel Purchas could even say that Jesus Christ was the true European.

> Europe is taught the way to scale Heaven, not by Mathematical principles, but by Divine veritie. Jesus Christ is their way, their

truth, their life; who hath long since given a Bill of Divorce to ingratefule Asia where hee was borne, and Africa the place of his flight and refuge, and is become almost wholly and onely Europaean. For little doe wee find of this name in Asia, lesse in Africa, and nothing at all in America [!], but later Europaean gleanings.[3]

Benedict, patron of Christian Europe. Well, I suppose a patron is one who provides the means by which the dreams of other men come true, and certainly, more than most, Benedict made possible the transmission of that great tradition of learning, in which the glory of Greece, the grandeur of Rome, the faith of Israel, and the wisdom of the Christian centuries were joined together. I was very glad to see the other day that in the parish church at Stratford-on-Avon, within a stone's throw of Shakespeare's grave, there is very properly a window of Saint Benedict. European culture between the sixteenth and eighteenth centuries is a kind of choral symphony in which one nation after another takes the solo lead: Italy, Spain, England, France, Holland, Sweden, Germany, Russia. But not simply an affair of growth and progress. It is a study in chiaroscuro of light and dark, of achievement and failure, above all, of struggle. The Protestant Reformation contributed notably to the shaping of Europe and it is generally supposed that this marked a halting of what we might call the Benedictine spirit. Well, perhaps that is so, and yet despite all his dire and drastic criticism of monasticism, Luther's priorities – God and conscience and the communion of saints – were those of Saint Benedict. Martin Luther went to the Diet of Worms for the same reason that Benedict went to Subiaco, because his conscience was bound by the word of God; God helping him, there he stood, for he could do no other. And the emblem of the beginning of the Protestant Reformation is a monk wrestling in prayer and studying his Bible, his unconscious mind teeming with the images and words of the Bible, and above all of the Psalms. Or John Calvin, the extrovert, but like Benedict, as Professor Léonard once said, the founder of a civilization, whose Christian community at Geneva John Knox praised in Benedictine terms as a most perfect school of Christ. And then John Wesley, who like Saint Benedict launched a great lay movement, a splendid missionary apostolate, binding together evangelism and education, whose Twelve Rules of a Helper, whose Rules for the Methodist Societies and whose Covenant service, are the nearest thing in western non-Roman Christianity to the Benedictine Rule; John Wesley who exercised a patriarchal authority over his communities, and bade them explicitly watch over the souls committed to them, those who must one day give an account. The lovely climax of the Rule of Benedict is almost exactly transcribed in a verse of Charles Wesley :

> Strangers and pilgrims here below,
> This earth, we know, is not our place;
> But hasten through the vale of woe,
> And, restless to behold Thy face,
> Swift to our heavenly country move,
> Our everlasting home above.

But there is darkness as well as light in the European story : the *Magnalia Christi*, but also a failure of nerve and obedience and compassion by Christian men. We have to reckon not only with involvement, but with estrangement, with what Paul Hazard calls the 'crisis of European Conscience', the way in which, as he said, most Frenchmen began the seventeenth century by believing the Christian faith with Bossuet and ended it by disbelieving it with Voltaire. And yet it is that Voltaire's Europe, as Federico Chabod has suggested, which is Europe come of age, Europe of artists, men of letters, sciences, academies, Newton, Locke and Galileo, Corneille and Racine and Goethe, that Europe of which Edmund Burke could say in 1796, 'No European can be a complete exile in any part of Europe'. We have to reckon, then, with the Europe of unbelief; of the eighteenth-century enlightenment and the fierce anti-clerical passion of nineteenth-century revolution. This is modern Europe. As far removed from Christendom as ancient paganism, but with its opening worlds of new learning and new patterns of human life, a world we cannot even comprehend simply in terms of the past, and which it would be foolish romanticism to suppose can be made Christian in the foreseeable future, if you think of Christian influence as a kind of glue sticking together the fragments of what was once a united world view, not forgetting the great crack down the centre, which we call the iron curtain. There is a famous cartoon of Max

Beerbohm about the last three centuries. There is the eighteenth century quizzically appraising his son, quite sure he cannot be the man his father was, and then the nineteenth century, fat, bespectacled, black-clothed, prosperous, beaming at his successor who is an even bigger, more prosperous more beaming edition of himself. And then the twentieth century, a young man with a black band on his arm, looking, not at his successor because he does not know whether he will have one, but at a great question-mark on the horizon. Perhaps if he had drawn that cartoon after the second world war, Max Beerbohm might have slightly altered the details and given us a teenager in jeans looking at a question-mark in the shape of a huge atomic cloud. There was another famous cartoon of Europe, done in the sixteenth century, which depicted Europe as playing its part in a terrible picture of the drunkenness of Noah. And it shows Japheth as the good son, piously averting his eyes from his father's shame. We can no longer take a 'holier than thou' attitude to Shem and Ham and their descendants. The sons of Japheth in our lifetime have slaughtered millions of their fellows in internecine strife. The common market to which France freely admitted us in 1914 and 1939 was a market in European flesh and blood. And what have we done, and what have we not done, to the sons of Ham? Is not the rationale and practice of apartheid in the end a European export and, I fear, a Protestant one? And what of the 'gleanings of Europe' towards the sons of Ham in Christian North America? What of the children of Shem, Israel and the Arabs, their fatal duelling pistols bearing the marks 'Made in Europe', the sons of Shem whose names we have written in blood in Auschwitz and Dachau and Buchenwald? We do not need Benedict as a patron. We need him very sadly and badly and urgently as a patron saint. Perhaps a modern cartoonist could still use the image of the drunkenness of Noah, showing our statesmen staggering from continent to continent, aimlessly and hopelessly.

> Far-called, our Navies melt away;
>   On dune and headland sinks the fire :
> Lo, all our pomp of yesterday
>   Is one with Nineveh and Tyre !
> Judge of the Nations, spare us yet,
> Lest we forget – lest we forget !

This is Benedict's real *patrocinium* – his intercession for us. If it were said of Burke's Europe that in no part of it could a European feel he was in exile, it must be said of Benedict's Europe that in every part of it a man is reminded that his dwelling is not here but yonder.

2

St Francis of Assisi*

W H E N , I N 1924, the coming of the first Franciscans to Canterbury was celebrated here, it was an ecumenical occasion. Of it, Paul Sabatier wrote: 'On communia en saint François.'[1] We too celebrate one whose praise is in all the Churches, whose memory is cherished by men from many religions and by those from none at all. Those who belong to the Franciscan Order have most right to speak, for they do so from within a continuing community life of more than 700 years. But from the beginning of the 'Francis renaissance' in the middle of the nineteenth century, others have made a real contribution: outstandingly the pastor from the Protestant heart of the Cévennes, Professor of the Protestant Faculty of Strasbourg, Paul Sabatier; but also a band of international scholars from many Universities and Churches – from Cambridge alone, F. C. Burkitt, David Knowles, Rosalind and Christopher Brooke, Bishop Moorman, Dr Gordon Leff.

In the military hospital of the Invalides, in Paris, the Emperor Napoleon Bonaparte lies in a majestic tomb of red porphyry upon green granite, surrounded by the Marshals of France and of the 'Grande Armée'. As Humpty Dumpty would say, 'There's glory for you!' But go from there to Assisi, to the little crypt where another 'Frenchie' – 'il francesco' – lies in his plain tomb in the grey travertine stone, surrounded by his companions, Brother Leo, Brother Masseo, Brother Angelo and Brother Rufino. No, *there* is glory for you! – the upside-down glory of the Kingdom of God.

What we know of Francis comes from a relatively few documents, the elucidation of which has been an intricate corner of medieval studies. At its heart, the few precious fragments like the autograph message to Brother Leo with its scrawly writing

---

* A lecture given in Canterbury Cathedral on 2 October 1976, on the occasion of the 750th anniversary of the death of St Francis

and bad grammar, and a few writings of his own which include
his Testament, and the Letter to Faithful Christians. In the main,
it is a collection of stories. None the worse for that.

> Tradition [wrote John Henry Newman] does not flow from the
> mouth of the half-dozen wise, or philosophic, or learned men ...
> but is a tradition of nursery stories, school stories, public-house
> stories, club-house stories, drawing-room stories, platform stories,
> pulpit stories.[2]

But stories get told and re-told and they swell in the telling.
They attract other stories, they become barnacled with corrobo-
rative details; in the case of Francis, from the Desert Fathers,
from the life of St Martin, from God's appearances to the
patriarchs in the Old Testament and from the stories of the
Temptation and Gethsemane in the New. And stories may have
their rough edges pared away to make them inoffensive, on
their journey from the lips of Brother Leo to the pages of St
Bonaventura.

On the whole we must be grateful that there are so many
which bear the imprimatur of his close friends – 'we who were
with him' – and others which by their ability to surprise and
even shock bear their own authenticity. For here are stories
pegged down in the real world of the Italian countryside, in sun
and rain and snow, summer and winter. Pinpointed in time and
place like the beginning to the story of Francis and the chirruping
cicada –

> One summer, when Francis was at the same house, staying in the
> furthest cell next to the hedge of the garden behind the house,
> where after his death brother Rainerius the gardner used to live![3]

And here is a way of life as startling to us today as it was
then, a company of men and women who seem to have less to
do with the ways of church-going Christians than with tramps,
squatters, stowaways – and even streakers, for some of the stories
have had breeches sewed on them as surely as Biagio da Casena
put them on the Michelangelo nudes in the Sistine chapel. The
famous 'Chapter of the Mats' must have looked more like a
Pop Festival than the General Synod of the Church of England
or a Methodist Conference.

The primary evidence about the conversion of St Francis must be his own words in his Testament :

When I was in sin, the sight of lepers nauseated me beyond measure : but then God himself led me into their company, and I had pity on them.

This is not to deny the much longer story with its three crises, which suggest not 'once at a crash Paul' but the 'lingering out sweet skill' of an Augustine.

We need not doubt the disillusioning effect upon the generous playboy of Assisi of his direct experience of battle, of prison, and of illness. When the would-be knight who rode out so bravely from Assisi returned alone and in secret, it may be because, when it came to the crunch, Francis had more of the troubadour in him than the soldier; and it would not, I think, be discreditable to suggest that he Caporetto-ed home, as a little later he would hide in a hole in the ground to escape his father's wrath. Authentic, too, the moment before the Cross in San Damiano and the call to rebuild the ruined church. And so to the great gesture of renunciation, marvellously captured for us by Giotto, when, naked, he publicly handed his clothes back to his father, Pietro Bernardone.

Francis is luckier than Martin Luther. The psychologists have not tried to make a rumpus with his father the main clue to an 'identity crisis'. And one wonders what would have happened had Bernardone, like Hans Luther, shouted at that moment : 'Have you never read in Scripture : Honour thy father and thy mother?' It would have had a point. If Francis entered religion from a broken home, it was he who had broken it. No doubt for the right reasons, and our sympathies, like those of the bystanders that day, are all on his side. But a good many parents, if they are honest, should have some sympathy with Hans Luther and Pietro Bernardone, whose plans and hopes for their children were no worse than the ambitions of most parents, and who came an awful cropper in trying to handle their sons. There is no word to say whether in later life Francis had qualms.

Certainly for him, henceforth, the word 'Father', which meant so much for Jesus, seems to have become a word on which his Brother Sun had ceased to shine. When he thought of relationship to his followers, it was the word 'Mother' which he chose, as is plain from his message to Brother Leo and from the guide-lines he wrote about hermitages, in which it occurs six times.[4] In part it was functional, as when we say round a teapot, 'Now who's going to be Mother?' But for Francis it goes deeper, and with his abundant use of 'Brother' and 'Sister' we may think that for him 'Father' was rather a spoiled word.

The drastic gesture of the naked Francis belongs very much to his times. The great F. C. Burkitt, who did so much for Francis studies, speaks for Englishmen when he confesses to a feeling that in those early days Francis was 'not quite sane' and that his preoccupation with suffering towards the end of his days was 'unnatural and unhealthy'.[5] But remember, too, the violent change in life style of Thomas Becket when he turned from Chancellor to Archbishop. Thirteenth-century Christians had not the advantage of a public-school education : they knew less about a stiff upper lip than a trembling lower one. And though Dr Burkitt (Harrow and Trinity) produced a fine and sensitive translation of Francis's 'Canticle to the Sun', by no stretch of imagination could St Francis have written the Harrow school song 'Forty years on' !

Then, swiftly upon conversion, vocation. Gerard Manley Hopkins once wrote, from his own experience :

> When a man has given himself to God's service and when he has denied himself and followed Christ, he has fitted himself to receive and does receive from God a special guidance, a more particular providence.

For Francis it came on St Matthias' Day 24 February 1206, when in the church of the Portiuncula he heard the gospel for the day :

> Freely ye have received, freely give. Provide neither gold, nor silver, nor brass in your purses, nor scrip for your journey, neither two coats, neither shoes, nor yet staves; for the workman is worthy of his meat.

But if Francis was born anew in utter nakedness, it was not in entire forgetfulness, but trailing clouds of mental glory. The French connection is of great significance. There are abundant references to the fact that, when deeply moved, Francis spoke and sang in a kind of French. This is more than the modish echo of a dominant French culture, as when the characters in a Turgenev novel break into French. In the South of France, in Provence and Aquitaine, there had grown up a brilliant, dangerously permissive society – where Muslims, Jews and Christians lived together, and where heresies of a rather deadly kind were openly countenanced. It was a brittle world, already on the way out – rather like the Deep South of America in the 1860s – and when there burst upon it the fury of the Albigensian crusade, when De Montfort's knights, like Sherman's cavalry, erased with fire and slaughter a brave world, overnight it was gone with the wind. A very dangerous place from which to borrow Christian thoughts, but safe for Francis because (perhaps following long talks with Bishop Guido) he was determined from the first to show complete obedience to the Church, complete loyalty to the Catholic faith. None the less it was a radical moment of secularization, in the best sense, when Francis drew boldly on Provençal culture, with its doctrines of chivalry and courtly love, the world of the troubadours who wrote poetry and the jongleurs who sang it. The evidence is overwhelming. Francis knew the Song of Roland, he knew about the Round Table – in their medieval setting, not that of nineteenth-century romanticism, which Manley Hopkins called 'playing the fool over Christian heroism'.

He rejoiced in the company of Brother Pacifico, a former troubadour, who had been crowned a Laureate of the Empire – a somewhat inflationary distinction, so that he was more of a Cliff Richard than a John Betjeman. He called his followers 'jongleurs', and from time to time would behave like one himself, drawing an invisible bow over an imaginary fiddle, and once even suggesting to a shocked Pacifico that he might scrounge a guitar.[6] Best of all, the moment when, called to preach before Pope Honorius III and his cardinals, he abandoned his sermon and began to speak with rising fervour, and, to the immense embarrassment of his patron Ugolino, and obviously also, of his biographer, 'his feet began to move as though he were dancing',[7] which we dare believe he really was! There is more here than the borrowing of techniques, as when John Donne turned the sonnet form to the praise of Christ. More even than the snatching of what we should call a model from another culture. It affected his life. Dr L. T. Topsfield, in his impressive study, *Troubadours and Love,* shows how the conception of 'courtesy', the very derivation of the word bespeaking its noble origins, embraces a coherent pattern of virtues : he shows, in the poetry of Marcabrou, that the true lover is endowed with 'jovens' – possesses generosity of spirit; 'valors' – moral worth; needs 'conoissensa' – discrimination between good and bad; needs the rational quality of 'mesura' – and all these united in the wholeness of 'cortesia', which is 'both the sum total of all the courtly virtues and their manifestation in social behaviour'.[8]

Here is something different from the catalogue of monastic virtues which from the time of St Benedict had spelled out the Christian way – obedience, humility, simplicity, discretion, and the like. For Francis, 'cortesia' is also a great word. He would have agreed with Hilaire Belloc :

> Of Courtesy – it is much less
> Than courage of heart or holiness;
> Yet in my walks it seems to me
> That the Grace of God is in Courtesy

We might almost translate it, Albert Schweitzer-wise, as 'Reverence for life'.

It was shown in his concern for the dignity of others : in a terrible moment when a young recruit shrieked out that he was dying of hunger – real or imaginary – Francis called for lights and summoned the brothers to a midnight feast;[9] or when he decided that ripe grapes were just what a sick brother needed, and took him in the garden and began first to eat, so that the brother might not be abashed.[10] And there is the moving story of the brother who in mistaken kindness took a leper for a walk into the town, where they met with such savage revulsion as to compel him to bring the sick man home, crushed with a traumatic experience of ostracism. Francis, who blamed himself, said, 'May this be my penance that I eat from the same dish with the Christian brother', and so a dish was put between the two.

The leper had sores and ulcers all over him and in particular his fingers, with which he ate, were contorted and bleeding, so that always, when he put them in the dish, blood flowed into it. . . . He who wrote this saw it and bore witness.[11]

But the supreme illustration of 'cortesia' is in that terrific moment when the doctor came to cauterize his forehead; when the instruments of this hideous surgery were white-hot in the fire, and when Francis's companions had fled,

> St Francis rose and said to the fire: 'My brother fire, noble and useful among all the other creatures which the Most High has created, be *courteous* to me in this hour, because I loved you formerly and still love you, for the love of the Lord who created you. I beseech our Creator who made you to temper your heat so that I may be able to bear it.' His prayer finished, he made the sign of the cross over the fire.[12]

It is in this light that his mystique about Lady Poverty is to be seen, for it is related to the tradition of courtly love. 'I have chosen holy poverty', he said, 'for my lady and for my bodily and spiritual delights and riches.'[13] It is a clue to his thought of Clare and her companions. They were to him not 'sorores' but 'dominae'. Dr Moorman says:

> Francis disliked the word 'Sister' altogether and refused to use it. He always referred to Clare as *Christiana*, the Christian'; and when one of the friars referred to the ladies as 'sisters' Francis was much upset and cried: 'God has taken away our wives, and now the devil gives us sisters.'[14]

It is surely no accident that when Francis as God's Troubadour composed his great Canticle of Brother Sun, it was in the company of Clare at San Damiano.

It is a pity that there are relatively few stories of the first years when it was bliss to be alive. Francis and his friends found Holy Poverty a source of happiness and joy. They identified, as we say, with the poor. As Fr Cuthbert has written,

> Poverty to him meant beggary: and we must not shy at the fact if we would rightly understand St Francis.[15]

But poverty and begging did not mean idleness. Francis worked, as he expected his men to work, with his hands. For the idle, the layabouts, the parasites, he had the most devastating of all his epithets – 'Brother Fly' ! Freely they received, freely they gave : the love of God, and the coats from off their backs. In his last illness, Francis, that worst of patients drove his nurses to exasperation by repeatedly giving away his bedclothes or his food the moment their backs were turned. David Knowles speaks of the 'absolute freshness and originality which were characteristic of his mind'.[16] Jean Guitton has written on the ways in which the Church may suddenly be 'young, original, forgiven – this creative élan can happen each time it is born from a movement, a society, a team and there is recaptured for one generation the atmosphere of the primitive church – one thinks especially of St Francis'.[17]

But we need also to remember what Christopher Brooke has said in his fine essay on 'Paul Sabatier and St Francis of Assisi' :

> His spontaneity was the product of a long training. The tricks, the pranks, the strange charades by which he bewildered his followers are surely in part a reflection of a deeper irony.[18]

Mrs Brooke has sensitively shown that Brother Leo stresses the order, the routine of this spontaneity, which becomes, like the rules of a sonnet, the vehicle of fervour. This is shown not only in his daily life and his reverence for the Church and its sacraments. It is at the heart of his 'imitation of Christ'. This is perhaps why he chose to remain a Deacon and so a Gospeller. It is said that when his sight was failing and one offered to read the Bible to him, he said he preferred to stick to the gospel for the day, which he always heard. And here his devotion to the Sacrament is all-important. He did not just read about the Jesus of history; he met him daily face to face in his Body and Blood. I expect like me you have stood in the Uffizi or the National Gallery and watched artists copying a great master. They spend a lot of time staring. So did Francis. As far as he could, he imitated the teaching methods of Jesus, though he had not, like Brother Giles, the gift for epigram. But he made up stories which really were parables rather than boring allegories, even though, like his Master's, they have got a bit mixed up as if they were jokes to which somebody has added different points. And he acted his teaching; as when he took Brother Masseo down a peg by turning him into a sort of whirling dervish, or silly schoolchild in the middle of the road, or sent the too reticent Rufino to preach naked in Assisi.[19]

Like some of the first Anabaptists he drew from a theology of the Cross what they called 'the gospel of all creatures'. Because he was forgiven, he knew that 'Christ had given him birth to brother all the souls on earth, and every bird and every beast should share the crumbs broke at the feast'. As Charles Péguy wrote of Victor Hugo, 'he had the gift of being able to see creation as if it had just come from the hands of its Creator'. But this was no abstract mysticism. G. K. Chesterton says:

> He is the very opposite of a pantheist. He did not call nature his mother; he called a particular donkey his brother or a particular sparrow his sister. If he had called a pelican his aunt or an elephant his uncle, as he might possibly have done, he would still have meant they were particular creatures.[20]

I have no doubt about the sermon to the birds, though I am not sure what was intended. If it was a sermon preached above the heads of the congregation, and if they had no idea what it was all about, then they were not the first or last to undergo such an experience. Perhaps it was the side effects which mattered. The Italians needed some such gesture who still annually slaughter birds on a scale next only to the British aristocracy in the month of August! And then, Christian art was never quite the same again. Professor Edward Armstrong's delightful study[21] deals in detail with the animal and nature stories, and shows that, while Francis had powers over animals and an understanding of them, his biographers had neither. Yet sometimes he shows a needless scepticism about incidents which have more modern parallels.

To talk to flowers, as Francis did, is today something of an 'in' cult: books have been written about it. I remember walking through St James's Park with a Rector of St Margaret's, Westminster, who raised his hat, as was his wont, to the Pelican who was his oldest parishioner. Professor Armstrong says that scared leverets do not run to human beings, as one did to Francis, but Martin Luther tells how some knights took him hunting, which he found a revolting experience, and how the hunted hare took refuge in his sleeves. Francis's reverence for Brother Worm

has its parallel in the churchyard at Eversley, where Charles
Kingsley put up a notice asking people not to tread on some worms
who had been befriended. Not for nothing did David Livingstone write on the cover of his *Journal*: 'He prayeth best, who
loveth best all things both great and small'. In it there is a fine
parallel to the story of Francis and the cicada. On that last
journey, Livingstone like Francis, weakened with fevers and
internal bleeding, sat on a tree in the pouring rain:

> As I sat in the rain a little tree-frog, about half an inch long,
> leaped on a grassy leaf, and began a tune as loud as that of many
> birds , and very sweet; it was surprising to hear so much music
> out of so small a musician.[22]

For a very likely story stripped of reverent frills I like best the
story of Brother Theobald who testified that while Francis was
preaching at Trevi, a donkey ran amok in the market-place and
suddenly stopped at the bidding of Francis – in the way donkeys
always unaccountably will, putting its head between its legs. And
'blessed Francis, in order that men might not take notice of a
miracle so stupendous began to say comic things to make them
laugh.[23]

Theologians had dwelt on the theme of man's dominion over
creation. Francis, like Jesus, thought of a God whose kingly
Rule consists in cooking dinner for the birds and sewing clothes
for the lilies of the field. 'Holy Obedience', he said, in a rather
enigmatic passage, 'renders a man submissive to all things in this
world, not only to men but even to wild beasts, so that they may
do their will with him in whatsoever way God may permit.'[24]

All creatures – and all the world. There is the Letter to All
Christians, in which he apologizes because, owing to illness, he
cannot visit us each individually! But it was an astonishing missionary impulse which sent his preachers into all parts of Europe,
and as far as China in an amazingly short space of time. About
his visits to Spain and to the Holy Land we should like to know
much more, but the sources fail. He was obviously unhappy
about what he saw of the Crusaders at Damietta and it needed
no charisma for him to prophesy that this profligate rabble could
not win their battle. There is great dignity on both sides of his
confrontation with the Sultan Melek-el-Kamil and I think he
may have offered to undergo ordeal by fire with the Muslim

holy men. Kamel might have blinded him and let him loose –
but what the courteous enemy did not do, his friend Brother
Sun seems to have done, for it is likely that the Palestinian sun
began the ruin of his sight.

And indeed we might call the months that followed 'The
clouding of Brother Sun'. He returned to sad tales of tensions
within the order, of action from above and from below which
would bring his movement into the greater service of the Church,
at the cost of Francis's drastic simplicities. There is no doubt of
the agony which it brought to Francis – which led him to cry,
'Who are these who snatch my Order and my brethren out of
my hands?'[25] Anger, too, when he found them building a house
of study at Bologna, or at Assisi, where he tore tiles from off the
roof.

Though there are, as Dr Brooke says, difficulties about the
story of the confrontation between Francis and Brother Elias at
Fonte Colombo, there may, I think, be a genuine core. There
must have been a moment when the clash became evident on a
small scale, among the inner circle. It is the story of how Francis
retired with Brother Bonizo and Brother Leo to re-draft his Rule,
and a deputation led by Brother Elias came to expostulate. Francis came down to meet them, and then turned from them to
call upon Christ, 'Lord, did I not tell you that they would not
believe you?' And then, says the story, the voice of Christ was
heard replying, 'I want the Rule to be observed as it is to
the letter, to the letter, to the letter, and without gloss, and
without gloss, and without gloss' ('ad litteram, ad litteram, ad
litteram, et sine glossa, et sine glossa, et sine glossa').[26]

So struck was F. C. Burkitt by the strange repetition of those
words that he made a special journey to the valley of Fonte
Colombo and found there what he had hoped to find :

> as a matter of fact there is a splendid echo : if you shout, so as
> to be heard down below, at least two syllables are repeated.[27]

So, as Francis angrily shouted, his words were flung back by the
reverberate hills. 'To the letter – and without a gloss !' You may
think this tells us more about the mental habits of a Modern
Churchman in the 1920s than about the thirteenth-century. You
may well ask whether the disciples did not know an echo when

they heard it. But this does not dispose of the question whether on that occasion Christ was speaking. Bernard Shaw puts some wise words into Joan's mouth when, in answer to her claim that her voices come from God, she is told bluntly, 'They come from your imagination.' 'Of course', she replies. 'That is how the messages of God come to us.'

To the next months belong those sad little stories with their headings 'in the time of his illness' – 'when his eyes were bad' : of a Francis only driven to take extra food or clothes, or even to consult a doctor, on holy obedience. Events move to the story of the Stigmata, for, as has often been said, the outward marks of the wounds of Christ did not come until he bore those marks already on his soul.

When a mystic tells us what he saw, the rest of us have a right, almost a duty, to discuss questions of 'subjective' and 'objective'. But when a saint says that he sees – the rest of us had better keep silence and let our words be few.

'Not reading and speculating, but living, dying and being damned, make a man a theologian', said Luther. An example of how men 'see' truth comes from the lovely prologue to the Seraphic vision – which tells how Leo, anxious about Francis, crept across the little bridge, overheard his prayers, and was betrayed by rustling leaves. Francis said to him : 'Know thou, friar, little sheep of Christ, that when I was saying the words thou didst hear, two lights were shown to me within my soul – the one the knowledge and understanding of myself : the other the knowledge and understanding of the creator.' Turn from this to two classic theological documents – to the opening of the *Institutes* of John Calvin : 'the whole sum in a manner of all our wisdom consists in two parts : the knowledge of God and of ourselves', and to the opening chapter of Newman's *Apologia*, where he tells how his evangelical training taught him to 'rest in the thought of two and two only supreme and luminously self-evident beings, myself and my Creator'.

If Catholic theologians have sometimes found ways to blur the challenge of Francis, Protestant theologians too have run away. They have talked about the theology of 'Imitation' as though it must inevitably be legalistic and outward, and have often sidestepped the problems posed by the Sermon on the Mount. But here I would take two rather Protestant points. The supreme vocation of Francis was not poverty but penitence. And out of penitence comes forgiveness, and from it joy, and from both come reconciliation. I remember in Eastern Germany the matron of a Lutheran hospital, which Russian soldiers had taken over, saying, 'We live from day to day and we live as a forgiven community.' It was as a forgiven community that the Franciscans became an instrument of reconciliation. It is perhaps why Francis claimed divine inspiration for his greeting : 'Peace be with you.'

About penitence there are two fine stories. The one, the saga of the importunate novice who pestered Francis with requests that he might have a psalter.

> Francis was sitting by the fire warming himself when the novice came yet again . . . Francis said to him : 'After you have a psalter you will want and hanker after a breviary; after you have a breviary you will sit in an armchair like a great prelate, saying to your brother : "Bring me the breviary." ' Thus saying, with great fervour of spirit he took some ashes in his hand and washed his head with them saying to himself 'Ego Breviarium! Ego Breviarium!'[28]

The other is the story of how Clare and her ladies looked forward to Francis's coming and his sermons as a great spiritual treat. And one day, as they sat back to listen,

> he ordered ashes to be brought, and having spread some of them on the ground in a circle round him he placed the remainder on his head.[29]

Then he suddenly stood up and recited the great Psalm of Penitence, Psalm 51, and abruptly left.

A man in dust and ashes says 'I am a breviary'. It was the age of magnificent tools of worship, the great cathedrals inspiring in their intricacy, an age of growing liturgy, beautiful and complex, of the making of Psalters, Gospel Books, Breviaries of rare worth. Yet here in Francis was the solemn reminder that in the end all these things are optional extras – meaningless without the devout heart, the joy of the forgiven soul.

> The tumult and the shouting dies;
> The Captains and the Kings depart :
> Still stands Thine ancient sacrifice,
> An humble and a contrite heart.

And because forgiven, a reconciler.

> His tunic was dirty, his person unprepossessing, and his face far
> from handsome [said honest Thomas of Spalato]. But God gave
> such power to his words that many factions of the nobility, among
> whom the fierce anger of ancient feuds had been raging with
> much bloodshed, were brought to reconciliation.[30]

'Peace be with you!' – a simple greeting, but its intensity shocked
those who heard it over the fields, and it was the very lively
Word of God accomplishing that whereto it was sent in Arezzo
and Perugia and Siena. Luther once said that it was a test of a
theologian whether he could relate Law and Gospel. There is a
deep problem here, which underlies the conflicts within the
Franciscan movement in Francis's last years and after his death.

Was Francis's highly individual life style with its drastic re-
nunciations a possible model for a great community? There is the
story of a housemaster upon whom some boys poured a jug of
water, and he mildly replied, 'What would happen if the whole
school did that?' It is a point to ask what would have happened
if the whole world, the whole Church, or even a great dedicated
community within it, adopted holy poverty, to the letter, and
without gloss, of Francis's rule. There is the further and distinct
point, that from the first there were spiritual failures apart from
the questions of practicality and in the next centuries it became
evident that the Friars Minor were also vulnerable to the temptations of wealth and power and popularity. Hence the difference
between the coming of the Friars to England and their going in
the sixteenth century, when many of them had become a by-word
for venality and greed.

But there is a deeper point. Francis notoriously could not
write Rules but only guide-lines – his famous counsel to Brother
Leo is in the end a refusal to give counsel: 'In whatsoever way
you think will best please our Lord God and follow him in his
footsteps and in poverty, do that.'

And here is something wider than religion. We all know the
phrases, 'He always goes by the book', and 'I threw the book at
him!' – and we groan when Brother Railway decides to 'work to
rule'. Taken by itself, the great point of Augustine's classic tract
Of the Spirit and the Letter is that Letter is something inert,
dead, apart from Spirit. It comes to life when the Spirit inspires

it. In their exegesis of Scripture, theologians like St Thomas intend by 'literal' the authentic meaning, the letter 'in the Spirit'. This has a most important consequence. If the Spirit is removed, what has begun as Gospel may end as Law : and what might seem to be Law may become Gospel if it is the vehicle of Spirit. And so those who seemed closest to Francis, to follow his first gospel, might end as the sour, bitter legalists, the 'zelanti' of the Franciscan spirituals, while those who seemed to have abandoned Francis's simplicity for more accommodating customs, could become fruitful for the Church in an order which produced saints like Anthony of Padua and Bonaventura, and an impressive tradition of spirituality and learning.

Let us return to where we began, the lower church at Assisi, every inch covered with painting of incomparable loveliness. Giotto, Martini, Lorenzetti, and Cimabue whose portrait of Francis seems almost a shy intrusion amid the triumphalism of these great descriptions of the apotheosis of a saint. The thought recurs – And what kind of glory is this? What has happened to the upside-down world of the Kingdom of God? Yet it might be said that Francis of Assisi in the end made the Church safe for Sister Art and Brother Learning, by putting them in their places and forbidding them to get out of hand, since at the heart of a great Christian civilization there stood this human question-mark against all its accepted values. Temperamentally, Francis had not much in common with Dean Swift, but on Swift's tomb in Dublin are the words which speak to us silently from the tomb of Francis – 'Dare you imitate him?'

There is the most poignant story of all, of how, thinking he was about to die, Francis called his companions and, slowly undressing before them, painfully lowered himself until he sat on the bare earth, and as they began to weep at sight of the frail body, ill and wasted, he added, 'Immediately my spirit has left my body, undress me completely, as I undressed myself before you, and put me on the bare earth and leave me there for as long as it would take a man to walk a mile.'[31]

It was the last, great, acted parable, complete when, on that October day, Francis welcomed Sister Death, and at the noise of weeping, the larks wheeled joyfully into the sky.

3

Luther: The Contemporary Image*

THAT TO EACH generation there is a different Luther, reflected and distorted in the mirror of the age, is commonplace among us in the light of the surveys of Luther literature throughout four centuries by Zeeden, Herte, Stephan, Otto Wolff, Bornkamm. One who looks back on the last twenty-five years of Luther studies may ask what images have been broken and made, and how has it gone with the quest of the historical Luther?

In the 1940s one image at least was shattered. Many of you have seen the striking picture of Dresden after the bombing, and of the statue of Luther, which had toppled from its pedestal face down among the rubble. A false image involved in terrible judgment? A Luther, if not Hitler's Spiritual Ancestor at least dangerously assimilated to what von Loewenich has called a 'deutsch-protestantischen Kulturprotestantismus'. Of this you can find traces even in Karl Holl, but by far the most striking evidence is the alteration made in Gerhard Ritter's fine study *Luther: Gestalt und Symbol*, between the first edition of 1925 and the fourth of the 1940s.

And then in the 1950s the Luther film, a Lutheran Luther, for the film moves to its climax in the founding of Lutheranism, and not improperly, since Luther's greatest creative achievement was to beget this mighty brood of Lutherans, his spiritual children, taught and trained by him along the way to heaven. A Luther serious and impressive, but in his belly not so much fire as glowing charcoal: obedient rebel, but perhaps more obedient than rebel, whose sonorous 'Eyn' feste Burg' is far from being a Christian Marseillaise. A Luther who has broken through from one orthodoxy into another, and not into some enthralling new dimension –

* The Inaugural Lecture at the Third International Luther Congress held in 1966 at Jäarvenpää, Finland

31

Like some watcher of the skies
When a new planet swims into his ken.

In contrast is the image of Luther in the '6os, in John Osborne's play, *Luther*. It is based on the most intelligent essay on Luther in English of our time, Erik Erikson's *Young Man Luther*[1] – a brilliant but one-sided and entirely unconvincing psychological study. But though Osborne's play, which shows Luther as an Angry Young Professor, is more lop-sided still, it has moments of genuine insight, and at least here is a Luther who is alive and exciting and who has moved history.

There was excitement that day. In Worms – that day I mean . . . he fizzed like a hot spark in a trail of gunpowder going off in us . . . he went off in us, and nothing could stop it, and it blew up . . . I just felt quite sure . . . nothing could ever be the same again . . . Something had taken place, something had changed and become something else, an event had occurred in the flesh . . . like, even like when the weight of that body slumped on its wooden crotchpiece and the earth grew dark.[2]

And I have another memory of an equally distorted image of Luther in the 1960s, the exhibition put on by the Communists, in the museum on the Wartburg, which showed Luther not as the religious prophet but as a supreme artist with words, a poet of genius, laying his impress deep on the shaping of the German language. Here too there is truth. I myself was drawn to read Luther by the beauty of the quotations from him in the footnotes to Karl Barth's *Dogmatics*. Luther has much more in common with John Henry Newman than most people realize – but certainly this, that both draw us not only because what they say is true but because at the same time it is profoundly beautiful and moving.

These public images of Luther have been haphazard and almost accidental. What of the serious, persistent search for the historical Luther, *Lutherforschung* and *Lutherdeutung*, which for concentration and scope ranks next to Biblical studies in the Protestant world? Two valuable essays by Walther v. Loewenich and Gerhard Müller show the diversity and range of Luther studies in the last twenty-five years.[3]

Some time ago, the Swiss historian, M. Dufour of Geneva,

accused me of portraying in the Cambridge Modern History a
Luther who has come straight down out of heaven. But so, of
course, Luther did. The exciting thing about human beings,
and a reason for the historical study of great men, is to seek the
'X' in their equation, the point at which they cease to be explained by heredity and environment and the thought world of
their contemporaries. In his famous sonnet to Shakespeare,
Matthew Arnold speaks of genius as being like a mountain, about
whose cloudy base men probe and search, but whose summit is
beyond them, open to the skies. His words are true of Luther,
too.

> Others abide our question. Thou art free,
> We ask and ask : Thou smilest and art still,
> Out-topping knowledge. For the loftiest hill
> That to the stars uncrowns his majesty, . . .
> Spares but the cloudy border of his base
> To the foil'd searching of mortality.

But, of course, it would be folly to think of Luther as unrooted
in and unrelated to history. If the theologian treats his ideas
seriously *coram Deo*, the historian is equally properly concerned
with his actions *coram hominibus*. It is most important that, to
use a quaint English phrase which Luther would have appreci-
ated, we look at Luther from a 'worm's eye view'. I hope that in
this present Congress we are going to do both these things.

It is becoming plain that some of the most important clues for
further Luther studies, as in the fifteenth century, are being held
up for lack of sufficient monographs and more clarification of
that complex religious and theological jungle of the half-century
before the Reformation, of which important areas are unmapped
and unexplored. Our present programme supports this view.
And here too we may pay tribute to the emerging edition[4] of
Luther's First Lectures on the Psalms.

We salute a team of splendid scholars, spanning two generations, proof, were it needed, of the recovery of German scholarship from the handicaps of the 1930s and '40s, as it is the crown
of the great Weimarana. And here we find support for the assertion that it is as we relate Luther most clearly to his context,
match his ideas most nearly with those of his contemporaries,

that we find more and more evidence of his freedom and independence and originality. In an age of melting labels, and the dissolving of categories, Lortz's 'Unklarheit' touches truth at this point; the way was open for this kind of independent breakthrough by Luther, and by others as well.

The discovery and editing, the publishing and the discussion, of most important documents and sources in this century has made it inevitable that Luther studies should be focused, almost obsessed, with the 'Young Luther'. Controversy has spiralled, as perhaps it will always do, about the question of Luther's breakthrough, about *Justitia Dei*. Ernst Bizer's 'Fides ex auditu' came as a kind of nemesis upon the hybris of some theologians who were beginning to regard this as a closed question and to speak of a consensus of agreement among scholars. We must be grateful to him for the depth and liveliness of his discussion, and not least for the important reminder that Luther did indeed rethink almost everything under the pressures of the great church struggle in those agonizing months 1517–21 when you might say of him, as G. K. Chesterton said of H. G. Wells, 'You can almost hear him growing in the night'. But this whole long controversy has pressed us back on the documents, has provoked first-rate essays, though anybody who has read them all from Vogelsang to Oberman must be a little like Bunyan's Valiant for Truth and say, proudly but a little ruefully, 'though with difficulty I have got hither, yet now I do not repent me of all the troubles I have been at to arrive where I am'.

Here I have only one comment and two footnotes to add on this theme. I am for an early date, before 1515. I cannot bring myself to believe that Luther's Lectures on Romans were written by one who was held up, blocked, cut off from the whole dimension of Paul's thought about the gospel. Then I think we ought to treat seriously Luther's reminiscence of 1545 to the effect that his new perception of the meaning of the *Justitia Dei* illuminated a whole set of other divine attributes which he now saw as dynamic, moving and given to men. He rejects, that is, as he later said, the view that God is related to the world like a sleepy nursemaid rocking a cradle with her toe, but here is a God who meets men creatively and dynamically in personal encounter. If this part of Luther's testimony is important then it bears on the date, for this doctrine is plainly evidenced in the

Psalms and Romans lectures. My second footnote is that Luther's problem lay within this one word *Justitia*. 'It's the single words that trouble me' is a genuine insight of John Osborne. It is not a question of combining *Justitia* with some other word like the divine *misericordia* – about which Luther had known all along. It is the search for the kernel inside the nut, within the notion of *Justitia*. And here, by way of illustration, I would draw attention to a word to which Professor Bornkamm has already drawn attention,[5] to the word 'Epieikia' or 'Aequitas', in German 'Billigkeit', in English 'Equity'. For this is treated as a part of justice itself in the 5th Book of Aristotle's Nicomachean ethics, on which Luther lectured and which he later singled out for special praise.[6] But here 'Epieikia' appears as a higher kind of justice, which intervenes in a special case, when universal justice and written law breaks down. And it is interesting that in English law this 'Equity' appears as an appeal from written law, directly to the conscience of the King. As far as I know, Luther never discusses 'Billigkeit' in relation to *Justitia*. The word becomes important for him in his discussions about earthly government in the 1530s and we could do with a monograph on his use of the word. If ever his lectures on Aristotle turn up, it would be interesting to see what he says about 'Equity' at this point. All that can be suggested is that this is an illustration of how complex is the conception, even in Hellenic usage, of *Justitia*, and how a double reference could lie within the single word.

I cannot here discuss the number of perceptive essays on Luther's theology of Justification and of his doctrine of the Church which have appeared in the last decades including some of the finest essays by such older scholars as Stange, Herrmann, Iwand, and a number of brilliant younger men.

I turn to the complex of problems beginning 'Luther and . . .', though perhaps 'Luther in . . .' would be a happier reference. I am one who is concerned about the danger to Reformation studies of over-labelling, of rigid typology, when it blurs distinctions, and draws attention from the particularities of history. This seems to me true even of the great labels 'Renaissance' and 'Reformation'. There is a certain tension observable between Reformation studies in Germany, Scandinavia and England and Renaissance studies in America, France and Holland. We are like men working from opposite ends of a tunnel and not quite meeting in the middle, and the gap is interesting. Modern studies seem to oscillate between overvaluing and underestimating the importance and originality of the humanists. What we need more clarification of is the extent of the common involvement and overlapping of humanists and reformers, the kind of investigation Dr Irmgard Hoess is conducting into the *Sodalitas Staupitziana* of Nuremburg, and of those men who were both humanists and reformers.

Among these assuredly is Luther, though not in the sense of a Spalatin, Melanchthon, Vadianus. But let us not minimize Luther's own store of classical learning. My colleague, Mr Marlow, of the Classics Department of Manchester, has tracked down the classical references on both sides of the controversy between Erasmus and Luther and he finds far more in Luther than in Erasmus. Of course, Luther's essay is by far the longer, but the allusions are frequent and often very subtle, so that this is not a case of Luther airing his classical knowledge, as Zwingli showed off by brandishing his Greek Testament about at the Marburg Colloquy. Recent writing on the German Bible has shown, as never before, how Luther eagerly and conscientiously used the latest humanist tools, especially the Erasmian New Testament. And when the young Professor Luther launched an educational revolution in the new University of Wittenberg, it was with the humanist slogan : 'The Bible – and the Old Fathers'.

The labels melt – humanists melt into schoolmen, from Pomponazzi to John Eck. But when we come to Luther and Scholasticism, there is a great transformation since some of us began our apprentice Luther studies by reading through the volumes of Denifle and Grisar, and even since Etienne Gilson was able to dismiss the later schoolmen as facile deviationists, falling away from the true scholastic norm, St Thomas Aquinas. The question 'Luther and St Thomas' still needs final investigation, and we have not yet decided how much Luther knew of genuine Thomism among the rigidities of the age of Capreolus. Let us not forget either that at Wittenberg too there were teachers of the *via antiqua*, that the first two publications of the new Wittenberg University Press were tracts from their Thomist lecturer – none other than Andrew Karlstadt – and that another of Luther's friends, Amsdorf, lectured on Duns Scotus. Even in a modern theological faculty, if we do not attend one another's lectures, we generally have some idea of what our colleagues are up to!

But the whole study of late scholasticism is in a fluid state. A series of brilliant essays, including those of Vignaux, Böhner, Iserloh, have shown the older classifications of Ockhamism, of the dogmatic historians, to be untenable, including the alleged too-sharp emphasis on the divorce between faith and reason. We have not yet, though Oberman is helping us to do so, assessed the significance of the dialectic of the *Potentia absoluta* and *Potentia ordinata*, the subtle way in which a doctrine can be turned upside down from an outrageous Pelagianism to a doctrine of created grace (and here a full study of the debate between Eck and Karlstadt at Leipzig might be very illuminating). Again, one wonders whether in the fifty years before the Reformation, and in view of the common ground between Ockham and Scotus, the labels *via antiqua* and *via moderna* have much meaning. What has been shown recently of the dependence of Peter D'Ailly upon Gregory of Rimini has drawn attention to the immense importance of the whole group, itself very diversified, of Augustinian theologians.

If we are far from the end of the discussion of 'Luther and ... Augustine', it is because we await the elucidation of Augustine's theology in the later Middle Ages. But at least as concerns Luther we are far away from the time when he could be dismissed, as by Denifle, as an ignoramus and a 'Halbwissender'. The editions of his early lectures, and such careful studies as those of Lohse, Oberman, and Leif Grane have shown beyond doubt that Luther knew what and whom and why he was attacking. And here, on another frontier, the labels melt between the schoolmen and the mystics. It has long been known that St Thomas counted for much in the long German mystical tradition from Meister Eckhart to Andrew Karlstadt, and perhaps also Thomas Müntzer. And Oberman and Landeen have drawn attention to the mysticism of Gabriel Biel.

Now 'mysticism' is perhaps the most nebulous word in the whole Christian vocabulary. It is a word which has fallen among thieves in its long journey from the Jerusalem of Christian sanctity to the Jericho of modern pantheist religiosity. Others will play the Good Samaritan in our Congress; it is rather for me, if not, like the Priest, to pass by on the other side, at least,

like the Levite, to take one shuddering glance and hurry on.
Here too, beware typology! Beware taking any one system, one
vocabulary, one process of salvation as though it were the touch-
stone of 'Luther and Mysticism'. Keep close to the citations, and
the documents, Augustine, Dionysius the Areopagite, Bernard,
the Victorines. Most of us would begin with the findings of
earlier scholars summarized recently by A. G. Dickens that
Luther

> was not impressed by the mental techniques through which the
> mystics sought to ascend the ladder of perfection to the higher
> states. Unlike theirs, his theology had no pantheist overtones
> and was altogether Christocentric. He would not follow the
> mystics into a passive abandonment before their sense of the vast
> and cloudy infinity of God. For Luther the tragic and triumphant
> sacrifice of Jesus . . . is central.[7]

What I would do is to call attention to what I prefer to
describe by an eighteenth-century term, to the renewal in the
later Middle Ages of 'inward religion'. This involved, in Germany, the conflation of two traditions. The first, that of the
'Modern Devotion', with its *Imitation of Christ* theology, coming
from Holland, and then, as Landeen has shown, infiltrating into
Germany through the Brothers of the Common Life, and touching the piety of such eminences as Nicholas of Cusa and Gabriel
Biel. But by 1500 the 'Modern Devotion' was not what it had
been : spiritual movements are generally rather tired in their
second century, and there is some evidence for the narrowing of
the 'Modern Devotion' at its latter end, in the puritanism of
Jean Standonck in Paris, and in the 'Anti Barbari' of Erasmus,
though his *Enchiridion* is a notable piece of evidence on the other
side, not least in its influence in Italy and Spain.

But alongside it, and mingling with it – and here such words
as 'Conformity with Christ' and 'Gelassenheit' are symptoms of
the merging – is the German mystical tradition : beginning in
the Rhineland with St Hildegarde of Bingen and St Elisabeth
of Schönau (Thomas Müntzer knew their writings!), a devotion
prophetic and apocalyptic, and the Thuringian mystics, the
Gertrudes and the Mechthilds with their concern for the sacred
humanity of Christ : the tradition which swells and becomes

fully articulate in Eckhart, Suso and Tauler. But here too is a piety which had seeped out into the world, beyond the cloisters. We need somebody to do for the 'Friends of God' in the late fifteenth century what Landeen has done with the *Devotio Moderna* – it has an important bearing on the origins of the radical Reformation. But here is a mysticism, if you will, which touched the minds of humanists, schoolmen, reformers. It is evident in the thought of Wimpfeling and Staupitz and their pupils. It affected some and not others – left the young Melanchthon untouched, it seemed, but deeply affected the mind of his fellow student, Johannes Oecolampadius : what other Martinian could have preached and published a sermon on 'The healing and the harmful winds that blow about the garden of the soul'?

Luther grew up in this world. His wonderful imagery of the immanence of God stems from this tradition. I have in mind the passages in his eucharistic confessions where he says that the whole God is wholly present in a leaf and in a nutshell, and the famous :

> Nothing is so small, but God is still smaller; nothing so large but God is still larger; nothing is so short, but God is still shorter; nothing so long, but God is still longer; nothing is so broad but God is still broader, nothing so narrow but God is still narrower, and so on. God is an inexpressible being . . .[8]

It is interesting to observe the effect of Tauler on Luther ('be-eindruckt' but not 'be-einflußt' is the plausible comment of Berndt Moeller) with his catastrophic effect on Thomas Müntzer, and the reasons why Luther edited and published the *Theologia Germanica* with the reasons for its deep impact on a whole series of radicals, beginning with Andrew Karlstadt. And then there is Luther's 'Theology of the Cross', those special stresses apparent between the first Lectures on Psalms and the Operations in Psalmos, 1519–21. Here are undoubted affinities with the tradition of 'inward religion' and yet the differences between Luther and others are more important than the similarities. And I suppose this too bears on the dating of the *Justitia Dei,* since one of the obvious reasons for the difference is that Luther moves within the world of the Bible and of Paul.

In speaking of Luther in relation to Karlstadt and to Müntzer, we have already touched the theme 'Luther und die Schwärmer'. Karl Holl's classic essay is still to be read with profit. Many of his intuitions have been supported by the vast weight of new evidence about Reformation radicalism which has become available in the last twenty years. A whole submerged continent has emerged from the sea, splendidly mapped for us in the breathtaking survey by G. H. Williams, solidly based on the evidence of masses of newly published documents. Of a great deal of this, Luther in Wittenberg was entirely ignorant, though whether, if he had known more, he would have liked what he knew any better is perhaps a question. He met at first hand the Zwickau prophets, but the creative importance of what has been called *Storchismus* has been exaggerated, and the evidence for Storch's doctrines is mostly very late. Andrew Karlstadt Luther knew only too well, and he came to look at all the Radicals through his own bitter experiences with one who, if not the Judas of Wittenberg, was at least its Alexander the Coppersmith. One remembers sadly the grim confrontation and dialogue between the two men in the Black Bear at Jena, two angry middle-aged men, Karlstadt almost beside himself with choleric rage, Luther coldly contemptuous as he tossed at him the golden guilder which was the badge of their public feud.

I revel in Luther's *Against the Heavenly Prophets*, and in the main am on his side. But it does not help Luther if we undervalue his opponents. One of the features of an age of revolution is that not only its great minds and men of genius are aware of what is new, but the second-class and second-rate figures also touch new truths. Among those dull, turgid, repetitive tracts of Karlstadt there are insights – it may be that he appealed to the supreme authority of Scripture before Luther, and was the first really to stress the priesthood of all believers in relation to the father of a Christian household. When we come to Luther and Thomas Müntzer, we come to a larger area of misunderstanding and mutual ignorance. There was no real confrontation between Luther and Müntzer (the notion that there was rests on a misreading of Luther, and I accept Müntzer's word at this point) and no real dialogue. Müntzer never understood the importance for Luther, too, of the dimension of existential *Anfechtung* for faith – and though there are differences, the similarities are paramount at this point.

And it is true of Müntzer also that once a Martinian always a Martinian : to the end, as Martin Schmidt has perceptively remarked, his is a Word of God Theology. It is likely that, as a liturgical scholar, Thomas Müntzer was in the Thomas Cranmer class and was more learned in this field, if more old-fashioned, than Luther and at least as skilful. Müntzer's Second Preface to his liturgies is a fine manifesto with genuine premonitions of the stresses of the modern liturgical movement. Luther himself recognized the merit of all this when he met them in disguise, in the work of their mutual friend, John Lang of Erfurt.

Luther's great perception is the all-embracing, creative dimension of faith – as some of the deep, seminal studies of our time, of Regin Prenter and of Gerhard Ebeling, for example, have shown us. Here is the creative centre of all Christian existence, the righteousness of God in Christ out of which we live *coram Deo* from beginning to end, a life always renewed in the Spirit from moment to moment. Peg it down, turn it into a process, map it out, and it becomes Law and not Gospel, Letter and not Spirit. I am not forgetting Luther against the Antinomians and the mass of edifying literature and institutions he created. But still he gives us a compass, and he does not, as later Protestant orthodoxy, draw a map. His is like some splendid painting by Turner of Venice in the clouds and sunshine : theirs is like a weather report from the Italian meteorological office. But Müntzer did draw a map, what later Protestants called a Plan of Salvation. He describes the stages of Christian experience and of our conformity with Christ. We may not much like his technical terms, but they are far from being mere pretentious jargon and mumbo-jumbo as Luther believed, and they supply a pattern which, in default of Müntzer, Protestantism had to invent again in Pietism and Methodism, and indeed Existentialism, for there is a startling amount of Müntzer that can be exactly paralleled in Søren Kierkegaard. So there is still room for discussion of 'Luther and Müntzer'.

I think I can understand why Luther could put Oecolampadius, and to a lesser extent also Zwingli and Bucer and Bullinger, among the 'Schwärmer', but modern research into the writings of these men have made it plain that here too we are beginning to reconstruct a more profitable confrontation and dialogue than was possible in the sixteenth century. And essays and books by Grimm and by Berndt Moeller have shown how important it is to pay attention to the background of the great cities of South Germany and Switzerland, though we still await a real elucidation of the differences between the Lutheran cities and those which turned to the emerging Reformed tradition.

And then, Luther and the theology of the Natural Order. Here we need not only to consider Luther's attitude to Natural Law, but in relation to 'Billigkeit', what we might almost call 'natural gospel', his stress on the spontaneous, inner, creative wisdom which the Creator God gives even to the heathen. And then, re-reading the essays by Lau and Heinrich Bornkamm, we have to consider what Luther has to say to the questions raised in our time by Teilhard de Chardin, to that D. H. Lawrence side of Luther which modern Protestants have politely passed over, as in that astonishing passage in the *Table Talk* :

> We are just beginning to recapture the knowledge of the creatures which we lost through Adam's Fall. We have a deeper insight into the created world than we had under the Papacy. Erasmus doesn't understand how the fruit grows in the womb. He doesn't know about marirage. But by the grace of God we are beginning to understand God's great works, and his goodness in the study of a single flower.[9]

The real ecumenical movement has hitherto been the conversation of the learned world, but now these things have more and more to be discussed within an ecumenical perspective.

The service which the Lutheran World Federation has done to Luther studies is a great service to the whole Christian Church, and it has unselfishly never interposed its quite proper confessional concerns and preoccupations on the world of scholarship. I hope this freedom will continue, for it is of the very essence of scholarship in a regimented age. I mean the freedom of scholars to discuss what they will when and as they will, to pursue some theme and turn to another and then to come back to the first. The great seminal studies of our time have not been in the main directed or commissioned dissertations, though I am all for keeping in touch across the world with what research is going on, and avoiding overlapping and wasted time. But for the rest let our motto be that to Nicodemus, 'Spiritus ubi vult spirat', rather than envying the Centurion, marshalling research students with 'Dico huic : vade, et vadit : et alii : veni, et venit'.

The dialogue between Protestants within the ecumenical movement cannot but be profitable for Luther studies. And of all the classic Reformers, perhaps Luther has most in common with some of the stresses of Orthodoxy, not least in the Russian Orthodox tradition (Luther and Dostoievski!). But it is the prospect of a resumption of the dialogue with Rome, broken off in 1543, which is the new and encouraging feature of the last decade. For four centuries there has been a tension between a Protestant Luther legend and a Catholic Luther caricature. Herte's volumes have shown how sadly persistent has been the long shadow cast by the attack on Luther, in his lifetime, penned by Johannes Cochlaeus. Even sadder, perhaps, is the remembrance that the author of one of the best modern studies of Luther, the late Giovanni Miegge, never published the second volume of his *Lutero*. I do not mean to ignore the value to Luther study of many Catholic writers in those four centuries, not least the writings of Denifle and Grisar.

But now we can put away our polemical blinkers, move even beyond the eirenically intended but perhaps pre-Vatican II studies of Congar, Bouyer, and Josef Lortz, who are still too concerned to show that what is true in Luther is not new, but medieval or at any rate Catholic. But the Vatican Council showed us the brave sight of the Roman Church beating our Protestant platitudes into Catholic epigrams, teaching us all new things about the Protestant Reformation. I was present in the Council when the statement on Indulgences was presented, a disappointing, conservative document which, had it appeared in 1517, might perhaps have reduced Luther's 95 Theses to 92, but hardly less. And then on the next day, Cardinal Döpfner, looking strangely like von Miltitz's dream of a Cardinal Luther in 1518, presented his magnificent counter-statement on behalf of the German and Austrian bishops, and how different this was. It went at points beyond Luther, not least in its Scriptural proofs.

The new methodology of dialogue, finely laid down in *De Ecumenismo*, the growth in charity and understanding, does not of course mean the end of debate and controversy. But it means that, on both sides, we can relax. It means, for example, that Protestants can write about Luther's faults without knowing that every admission will be used as polemical evidence against them. The great Protestant essay on the limitations of Luther has yet to be written! We admire Luther's inflexible and unyielding integrity in loyalty to the Word, his concern to bear his witness to the Truth at all costs. And we are all grateful for Pelikan's fine essay on Luther's intermittent eirenical adventures. But I think we have to ask whether Luther (and not Luther alone, but most men of his age) did not pass on to his followers a view of pure doctrine and its relation to error which was not that of the mind of Christ, but which in fact appeared in the late second century, and from which the Churches in our time are struggling to be free.

I hope we remember Heinrich Bornkamm's words at Aarhus, that we must not let the intriguing preoccupation with Luther's theology distract us from the tasks of the historian and the biographer. We still wait for a full, learned modern study of the mature and ageing Luther. Nobody can read the life of Winston Churchill by his physician, Lord Moran, without being aware of the effect of physical infirmity on a noble mind : the long list of Churchill's illnesses is curiously like that of Luther's in his last decade, and we have to ask questions of the effect of these things on Luther's mind and judgment, virile and sensitive as it was to the end. But we must have the whole Luther, warts and all : the sublime intuitions, and also the obtuseness and the limitations. Let us adventure more boldly into the discussion of the quality of that mind, its limitations which he shared with his contemporaries, and some of which perhaps were limitations peculiarly his own. We shall still have a Luther whose head is among the stars, the one who still exercises this wonderful magnetic pull across the world, drawing us from the far corners of the earth to sit at his feet, and learn from him. This is an age which sorely needs all the giant voices of the past, which needs more than most perhaps this Doctor Evangelicus, one who points beyond himself to God, at once both hidden and revealed, *Deus crucifixus* – and the triumph of his Cross.

4

Thomas More and William Tyndale*

THOMAS MORE was no mean Londoner. He found the
names of the City streets as evocative as a battle roll. If he had
an Oxford wit, he had a Cockney sense of humour, not least in
a certain dead-pan quality. In turning to law he followed in his
father's footsteps, and perhaps the thought of his father's pride
and pleasure may have had something to do with his decision to
become Lord Chancellor. He came to the Inns of Court, one of
that great company of articulate Christian laymen who were to
make the Inns the great preaching audience of the time. As a
common lawyer and an advocate and as one occupying legal
posts in government, he found in law his true craft, and it came
to colour all his mind. By its side, sometimes challenging it in
his affection, was a love of learning and of letters, his place of
eminence in that humanist circle which included Colet and Tunstall and Erasmus. It was as friend and collaborator of Erasmus
that he turned to satire, in that significant translation of Lucian
which Mr H. A. Mason expounded a few years ago in a brilliant study too little known.[1]

With his friend Colet, More stood gratefully within that
Augustinian Platonist tradition which had been a great succession
in medieval Oxford, and of which his London lectures on 'The
City of God' and his little life of the Florentine Platonist Mirandola were an emblem. He had a mind richly imaginative, as his
History of Richard III shows: deeply compassionate, as his
analysis of England's ills in the beginning of the *Utopia* reveals,
and his tender humour is over all his works. But lawyer, scholar
– there were other pulls. Brought up in Cardinal Morton's household, he was early aware of the possibilities of learning and
advancement in the service of great men, and became more and
more involved in affairs of state, and of the court,

* A Lecture given in Cambridge as one of a series on 'Men of Influence'
arranged by the Divinity and Education Faculties

becoming successively Under-Sheriff of London, Master of Requests, Privy Councillor, Knight and Speaker of the House of Commons, High Steward of each University in turn, Under-Treasurer, diplomat, Chancellor of the Duchy of Lancaster, and in 1529 Lord Chancellor of England. No wonder that from afar it seemed that, as Fuller says of somebody else, he was man of much motion and promotion, one who from modest beginnings had gone right to the top, so that, to unfriendly observers like William Tyndale, he seemed a man on the make, a career diplomat greedy for office like so many in a venal age.

So his career might seem, from without. Within, it was another matter. Here the crisis was not, 'Lawyer, or letters, or the Court?' but rather the call to leave the world for a life of discipline and contemplation. He spent many months as a layman in the Charterhouse, pondering this choice. I take seriously the words of Erasmus that when More 'found he could not overcome his desire for a wife he decided to be a chaste husband rather than a licentious priest'. He did not wear a hair shirt for purely ornamental purposes. He was a man of deep emotion and strong imagination. His second marriage, within weeks of his first wife's death, may be another clue. To see him as a religious *manqué* who had really agonized over the decision helps me to understand what has puzzled many, the way in which Luther's marriage, described in the most contemptible terms, occurs scores, perhaps hundreds, of times on page after page of his polemical writings – the breach of vows, the marriage of a monk with a nun – to be explained only in terms of the basest motives – what would otherwise be a Mr Dick's King Charles head, an almost pathological obsession, becomes explicable if it touched a chord in his own life – Luther was not only playing foul but wrecking the very rules of the game! I would not press the point but it is not in any way to his discredit to suppose that More was, like the man in the song, 'a rather susceptible Chancellor'!

History says he made the wise choice. His home and family at Chelsea was not only among his chief joys but the marvel and envy of less happy friends. When his cup of happiness was filled to the brim, it was his daughter Meg who filled it. His answer to the question, 'Why come ye not to court?', would have been that court life was vain and boring in comparison with home. Dr Dermot Fenlon in his recent skilful and profound lecture (published in the Transactions of the Royal Historical Society, 1975) has suggested that More saw in his home the emblem of true community, that against the background of the monastic *familia* and in the context of sixteenth-century cities, it is a clue to the meaning of *Utopia*. He might agree that More's household could be paralleled in the homes of humanists like Conrad Peutinger with his learned daughters, or reformers like Martin Bucer, to say nothing of Little Gidding and many Puritan homes thereafter.

From 1517 he became fatefully involved in what in his *Richard III* he referred to as 'Kings' games' in sadly prophetic words :

> These matters be Kings' games, as it were stage plays, and for the most part played upon scaffolds. In which poor men be but the lookers-on. And they that be wise will meddle no further. For they that sometime step up and play with them, when they cannot play their parts, they disorder the play and do themselves no good.

I do not doubt that More accepted gladly the office of a king's servant, nor that he accepted his personal friendship with something of the romanticism of a Renaissance courtier for his Prince. Nor is there much doubt that Henry counted him as more than his spare secretary, his go-between with Wolsey, more than just his tame humanist, whose brilliance and wit rubbed off on his own reputation. But I do not think More had many illusions despite the glamour – 'If my head could win his Majesty a castle in France, it should not fail to go.'

More had compassion about public ills – the decay of husbandry, and of towns. When his barns at Chelsea were burned during his absence at court, and his own corn and that of his neighbours was destroyed, it was of his neighbours that he thought, and he wrote to his wife :

> I pray you to make some good ensearch what my poor neighbours have lost and bid them take no thought therefore, for, and I should not leave myself a spoon, there shall be no poor neighbour of mine bear no loss, by any chance happened in my house.

In public office he was the King's servant, and more concerned to defend government policy than with mental fight to build Utopia in England's green and pleasant land. It was in the fight against Luther that he and the King became close collaborators, a relationship intimate enough to become dangerous when Henry opened to him the grave matter of his broken marriage. When he accepted the Chancellorship he must have known the frightful dangers ahead, but Henry VIII made him an offer which he could not in the nature of things refuse. Lord Hailsham has recently said that it is no part of the office of a Chancellor to act as inquisitor – though More used his influence to greater effect than Wolsey in supporting the bishops in their attempt to stamp out a heresy which was, as he said, 'spreading like wildfire' – but if as Chancellor he could do little he gave strong moral support and took part in the grim investigations. He fulfilled wholeheartedly the apologetic task committed to him by the bishops, first to read and then to refute the more dangerous heretical writings coming into England from exiled reformers. He was a layman, perhaps too simplistic and unaware of the intricacies of his themes, that there were for example far more theological arguments of fifteenth-century theologians which came near to Tyndale's definitions. But there are times when common sense and humour – G. K. Chesterton and C. S. Lewis come to mind – more than compensate for lack of technical theology. As a collector of theological dog-fights, and as one who has had a nibble or two in his own right, I rate More's first *Dialogue* and Tyndale's *Answer* fairly highly. They are both at times superbly written and More deploys all his great range of wit, devotion and insight. Of course, he writes as a lawyer, as a skilful advocate who makes concessions only on inessentials, who makes illusory gestures to the opposition, who ignores altogether the defendant's criminal record, who always puts the worst interpretation on what his opponents say. I suppose most of us have a point of deep conviction, however humorous or compassionate we may be, when humour and compassion wither, and this More reached in the weary, boring and interminable *Confutation* which followed.

He is [as C. S. Lewis says] monotonously anxious to conquer and to conquer equally at every moment : to show in every chapter that every heretical book is wrong about everything, wrong in history, in logic and rhetoric and in English grammar as well as in theology – to rebuke magnificently is one of the duties of a great polemical writer. More often attempts it, but he always fails.

His references to the men he helped to arrest, torture, burn, are indeed drained of compassion and even of humanity. Only in that last ninth book, when he himself was nearing the shadows, is there a change of mood, and there are those revealing words:

> And yet, Son Roper, I pray God that some of us, as high as we seem to sit upon the mountains, treading heretics under our feet like ants, live not the day that we gladly would be at league and composition with them, to let them have their churches quietly to themselves, so that they would be content to let us have ours quietly to ourselves.

For now More was beset by great danger. The divorce was past, but now came the attack upon the clergy, and Dr Elton has noted that More's resignation followed hard upon the submission of the clergy in 1532.[2]

In letters to Erasmus and to Cochlaeus, More pleaded that the reason for his resignation was ill-health – a modern enough excuse for disappearance from office in a totalitarian regime. I do not doubt More's ill-health, but if you read the lines carefully there is, I think, a deliberate ambiguity – 'I suffer from pains in the chest' – but the word is 'pectus', and it can mean 'heart' or even 'conscience'. When he goes on to say that it is going to be a long business ('and I don't know if I shall come out of it alive') one wonders, at a time when all correspondence of More's out of the country might be intercepted, if he is not hinting to his friends of the dangers of the new situation. For here is perhaps the point which marks him off from Erasmus. Richard Ullmann, a modern German Quaker who survived the concentration camps, said to me about the outburst of satirical writing in Germany after 1945: 'Satire is the last refuge of those unwilling to face the Cross.' Beyond Lucian, and the *Utopia* and *The Praise of Folly*, there was a situation which Erasmus recognized when he made that cold comment on hearing of the death of Thomas More, 'He should not have got entangled in dangerous affairs, and he ought to have left theology to the theologians.'

In his splendid article on the Trial of Sir Thomas More in the *English Historical Review* Dr Duncan Derrett showed how More the lawyer defied the law without subverting its dignity.

> Law was law, even if by standards of eternity it was wrong. This attitude is exactly what one would expect from More's career, his own training and mentality : his conscience was his own affair : it might have been better if the law of England had agreed with him, better for him and, he believed, better for the nation, but even if it did not, it was still the law.

There is a remarkable modern parallel. One of the noblest figures in the German Resistance in the second world war was Helmuth James Count von Moltke.[3] With so many Prussian generals and Field Marshals in the family he was almost inevitably a pacifist, and he refused, with sound Christian instinct, to take part in the plots to assassinate Hitler; and so he stood apart from his colleagues, much as More from Fisher and the Carthusians. Von Moltke too was a lawyer, and he too skilfully used the weapon of silence – 'he insisted on his own non-participation – he had only thought'. But at the end, after the farcical trial, after he had been hanged with a piano wire, the judge scrawled across the papers : 'He did more than think.'

More skilfully evaded being involved in the affair of the Nun of Kent, in which John Fisher was sadly compromised. But with the oath acknowledging the Royal Supremacy, and with the Act of Succession involving it, he had reached the point of no return. Robert Bolt, in his fine play, must as a dramatist divide his characters into 'goodies' and 'baddies' – but in those dark corridors of power all cats were grey, and though I suppose Richard Rich may have been even more odious in fact than in fiction, More himself never makes charges against Anne Boleyn, Cromwell, the Duke of Norfolk. At the last, what counted was the implacable anger of one man, his Prince.

In his famous novel *The Silences of Colonel Bramble*, André Maurois sugested that it was the long silences of a British colonel, as he sucked his pipe, which were the most eloquent thing about him. Sir Thomas More too elected silence : the letters he would not read; the questions he would not answer; the assurances he would not give; the statements he would not utter; the oath he would not swear. It was a lawyer's weapon, used with consummate skill, and it almost saved him. For Von Moltke and Thomas More did more than think. Both men, in the very act of using, of upholding the law, quite surely saw behind all the fine façade the will of a tyrant whose ruthless egoism meant in the end the finish of all law, all justice. Here was their protest, here their achievement.

It was in the end an affair of conscience :

> In my conscience [said More] this was one of the cases in which I was bounden that I should not obey my prince.... In my conscience the truth seemed to be on the other side – wherein I had not informed my conscience neither suddenly or lightly but by long leisure and diligent search for the matter. I leave every-man in his own conscience and methinketh that in good faith so were it good reason that every man should leave me to mine.

But, as Dr Elton has said, 'by his part in the events of 1529–34 More had made sure that his conscience could not in the end be left private to himself'.

For conscience is indivisible – most private and, by the very fact, a public thing. No doubt More would have defined conscience in fourteenth- and not in nineteenth-century terms – of St Thomas or Jean Gerson. But we should remember John Henry Newman; who wrote :

> If I am obliged to bring religion into after-dinner toasts I shall drink – to the Pope, if you please, – still, to Conscience first, and to the Pope afterwards, having said earlier : Conscience ... is a messenger from Him, who, both in nature and in grace, speaks to us behind a veil, and teaches and rules us by His representatives. Conscience is the aboriginal Vicar of Christ.[4]

Newman himself said that he shared this view of the authority of conscience with the dissenters of his day. At the height of the Parnell crisis, the Methodist Hugh Price Hughes spoke for that nonconformist conscience when he quoted John Bright : 'We stand immovably on this eternal rock. What is morally wrong can never be politically right.' A dangerous denial of the art of the possible ? But it also proclaims the indivisibility of private judgment and public behaviour. After his silence comes the eloquence of More's death. Therefore ask not for whom the bell of St Peter ad Vincula in the Tower tolled on that day. It tolled for all of us. It bears witness than conscience doth make heroes of us all, or if not of all of us, of a long succession of just men from Micaiah the son of Imlah to Thomas More and Helmuth James von Moltke. For what the tyrants and the persecutors always forget is the truth pronounced by Søren Kierkegaard : 'You can silence a living man. But when a dead man speaks, who can silence him?'

Rudyard Kipling, in his story 'Proofs of Holy Writ', shows Will Shakespeare and Ben Jonson, sitting in an orchard, talking and munching fruit, when a messenger arrives with a bundle of papers, proof sheets of the new English Bible; and Shakespeare walks up and down as together they revise the sixtieth chapter of Isaiah, polishing each phrase until it begins to sing with the cadences we know so well – 'and thy God thy glory'. The point is plain : only a master of words, only one with a poet's feel for our language could have produced the English Bible. William Tyndale was such a man.

William Tyndale is part of Oxford University's slender contribution to the English Reformation. In the battle he found raging between the humanist 'Grecians' and the reactionary 'Trojans', he and Thomas More were on the same side against the Scotists and 'like draff' and in support of the study of the sacred languages. His upbringing and his early career as a young parson was in those western midland parts which had old links with Wycliffe and with Lollardy; and I think, more than I would have thirty years ago, that he owed something theologically to Wycliffe's ideas (though not perhaps to the study of the Wycliffe manuscripts). He came to stress, as did Wycliffe, the decline of the Church through the poison of great possessions, the sins of clerical covetousness, of clerical infiltration into positions of temporal power, and of clerical use of violence.

For him, as for John Wycliffe, it was a primary definition of the Church that it consists of the Elect, and like Wycliffe he spoke of the gospel as the 'law of Christ' (an ancient description and not legalistically interpreted) : his use of 'law' is within the orbit of the love of God and of one's neighbour, as Wycliffe had beautifully expounded it in his exposition of the Ten Commandments – 'The Divine Mandates' – and Tyndale is here nearer to Wycliffe than to later Puritanism. The godly merchants who subsidized his study, men like Richard Hunne and Humphrey

Monmouth, and the Essex country folk who bought his New Testament, were members of companies which had survived from Lollardy. His prentice translation was the *Enchiridion* of Erasmus and he was powerfully impressed by the Erasmus New Testament of 1516, the new Greek text and the new Latin version and not least by its Preface with its bold plea for an open Vernacular New Testament, so that the ploughman might read the gospels at his plough and the weaver at his shuttle, and maybe even commercial travellers might learn to tell these tales to one another. Rebuffed by Tunstall who may have sensed warily that here was more at stake than humanist philology, Tyndale went abroad, and once he had left England it became more and more dangerous to come home. At least two of his friends were burned when they were caught on tip-and-run raids back to England. In the late 1520s, when contraband literature was coming into the country thick and fast, there was grave danger for all involved in smuggling books on behalf of the German Connection.

Exile was the oldest punishment for heresy and we ought not to underestimate the pain of it, poignantly described by a succession of writers from the Anglo-Saxon poets to Solzhenitsyn, badgered from pillar to post – 'everywhere and nowhere' as Sir Thomas More said – moving and covering his tracks so successfully that to this day they have not been uncovered. Unlike Luther and Erasmus, he could never count on a loyal and competent team of helpers. Those two theological clowns, William Roye and Jerome Barlow, roamed up and down the Rhine, leaking scurrilous poems, which disgusted Tyndale who thought that 'it doth not become the Lord's servants to use railing rhymes' – George Joye was even more irresponsible and as slap-happy as Erasmus' helpers Oecolampadius and Gerbel, who took out his readings and substituted an apparatus criticus of their own : only at the end, he had the help of John Rogers and Miles Coverdale. What was needed at first was a faith in the English language :

They will say, it cannot be translated into our tongue it is so rude. It is not so rude as they are liars. For the Greek tongue agreeth more to the English than the Latin. And the properties of the Hebrew agreeth a thousand times more with the English than the Latin.

He used what tools he could get in the way of dictionaries, and above all Luther's Bible and Erasmus' Testament. Before he had done, the hunt was on. Of that first quarto of 1525 of 3,000 copies only one fragment, consisting of the first twenty chapters of St Matthew, has survived. The only complete (and that not quite complete for it lacks the title page) copy of the 1526 New Testament is in Bristol: the only one of 6,000 to survive – a lovely little book, the pages still shining, so that it was evidently concealed and treasured rather than read. We shall never know how near the whole venture was to complete destruction, how tempted Tyndale may have been to stop. For every reader of the book would be in danger.

> Let it not make thee despair, neither yet discourage thee, O reader, that it is forbidden thee in pain of life and goods or that it is made breaking of the king's peace or treason unto his highness to read the word of thy soul's health.

This was the work which he polished and revised, again and again before the final edition of 1534 appeared, which was his seminal masterpiece.

Of the integrity of his intentions there can be no doubt. With all his heart he meant what he wrote to his friend John Frith :

> I call God to record against the day we shall appear before Our Lord Jesus, to give a reckoning of our doings, that I never altered one syllable of God's Word against my conscience nor would this day, if all that is in the earth, whether it be pleasure, honour or riches, might be given me.

In the little preface which appeared as an epilogue to the 1526 edition he invited

> those that are better seen in the tongues than I, and that have higher gifts of grace to interpret the sense of the Scripture and meaning of the spirit, ... if they perceive in any places that I have not attained the very sense of the tongue or meaning of Scripture, or have not given the right English words that they put to their hands to amend it.

Every translation of the Bible from Jerome's Vulgate to the N.E.B. has been greeted with howls, and Tyndale's was no exception. Three thousand blunders, cried Tunstall – of a text, at least 75 per cent of which would survive for centuries in the Authorized Version. But in Tyndale's case there were other charges : there were some Prologues and Marginal Notes, most of which came from Luther's Bible. It was perhaps not the wisest thing to have done, and later editions discarded them. But some sort of marginal notes were needed in an age without commentaries, and the majority are bits of philological and geographical information, while there is nothing more scurrilous than some of the notes in Erasmus' Testament. And Luther's Prologues are descriptions, about the common core of the gospel, the great evangelical stresses. It is true that the famous six ecclesiastical words, 'charity', 'church', 'do penance', 'priest', 'confess', 'grace' were shockingly changed, and Tyndale's words, while philologically defensible, had an eye to what he believed to be the perversions of contemporary authority. But three of the six you will find today in the Jerusalem Bible, another in the N.E.B., while the others have behind them the authority of Laurentius Valla and Erasmus.

A year or so ago, on the Wartburg in Eastern Germany, the Communist authorities put on a splendid exhibition about Luther's Bible. They had no sympathy at all with his beliefs, but they portrayed Luther as the great poet, the man whose magic mastery of words was a formative influence on the German language itself, striking deep into the literature, life and religion of the German people. We owe it to Tyndale more than to anyone that, like the German Bible and unlike many other Bibles, unlike the first New Testament, our English Bible is a work of majesty and beauty. I will not attempt to say what so many have said across four centuries of the impact of his words on our literature, our poetry, our proverbs, our religion and our life-style. And not on our nation alone. The English language still bestrides the world – hanging over it like the grin on the face of the Cheshire Cat, after the British Empire has disappeared !

Sir Thomas More might rustle up all the arguments which had been used since Archbishop Arundel forbade new translations in 1408 : the old metaphors about how dangerous it was to put a knife in the child's hand, of the need to keep a cover on the well lest the younglings fall in; his own plan that the Bishops should dole out copies to trustworthy laymen – here a gospel, there a gospel – with an 'X' certificate for the 'Epistle to the Romans' because of its difficulty and problems. More and the bishops were not far wrong in regarding Tyndale's New Testament with horror as a nuclear device which might make all the difference in the war against an imminent revolution. Through Tyndale the English Bible became the most important single fact in the ultimate, religious, Reformation. It struck into the minds of men at every level of society, in every walk of life. But for it, it is unlikely that the Reformation could have survived the pressures of political power and economic self-interest or that the great preachers, Latimer, Knox, Bradford – the goodly fellowship of the prophets, or the noble army of martyrs – Cranmer, Hooper, Ridley – could have won their day.

Of course, there was more to it than accurate text and philological investigation. There was a view of the contents of the Gospel. But in chopping Tyndale's butterfly to live bits and looking at it, piece by piece, under a polemical microscope, Sir Thomas More hardly saw it. He never really listened to Tyndale. There is a splendid devotional book, *The Heart of Thomas More*[5], in which passages from his writings are arranged for each day of the year. There are, similarly, one or two pieces which are the 'Heart of William Tyndale'. In the first place, the priority of grace, the divine initiative in our salvation :

As though we first sought out God ! Nay, God knoweth his and seeketh them out and sendeth his messengers unto them and giveth them an heart to understand – Did the heathen or any other nation seek Christ? Nay, Christ sought them out.

And the beautiful lines :

Who taught the eagles to spy out their prey? Even so the children of God spy out their Father and Christ's elect spy out their Lord and trace out the paths of his feet and follow, yea though he go upon the plain and liquid water which will receive no step and yet there they find out his foot : his elect know him.

And behind this is Tyndale's own experience :

Faith cometh not of our free will, but it is the gift of God, given us by grace . . . and why God giveth it not every man I can give no reckoning of his judgments ... but well I wot I never deserved it nor prepared myself unto it : but ran another way contrary in my blindness and sought not that way but he sought me and found me out and showed it me and herewith drew me to him. And I bow the knees of my heart unto God night and day that he will show it to all other men and I suffer all I can to be a servant to open their eyes.

To love the law of God and profess it so that thou art ready of thine own accord to do it and without compulsion is to be righteous ... and so much as he lacketh of love towards his neighbour after the ensample of Christ so much he lacketh of righteousness.

Saint-Saëns once said of his own music that the tunes came into his mind as easily as apples grow on apple trees, and this is the way both Luther and Tyndale think about good works:

Where the Spirit is, there it is always summer and there are always good fruits – that is good works.

Where an apple tree is not, there can grow no apples.

Right faith is a thing wrought by the Holy Ghost in us which changeth us and turneth us into a new nature and begetteth us anew in God ... it is a lively thing, mighty in working, valiant and strong, ever doing, ever fruitful : so that it is impossible that he who is endued therewith should not work always good works without ceasing.

Here, as against all legalistic Puritanism, is the true Liberty of a Christian man. The legalist,

because the love of God and his neighbour is not written in his heart, therefore in all inferior laws is he beetle blind ... the holy day will he keep so strait that if he meet a flea in his bed, he dare not kill her ... and in ceremonies he looketh ever with a pair of narrow eyes and with all his spectacles upon them lest aught be left out.

It is Sir Thomas More who is the Sabbatarian, and Tyndale who says :

We be Lords of the Sabbath and may yet change it into the
Monday or any other day as we see need ... we may make two a
week if it were expedient and one not enough to teach the people.

It is Tyndale who stresses the Christian's liberty over buildings
and places.

It is the heart that worshippeth God and not the place. The
kitchen page turning the spit may have a purer heart to God than
his master at church and therefore worship God better in the
kitchen than his master at church.

From this comes a root of Christian democracy. Thomas
More, *Utopia* apart, talks about women and wives much as a
music hall comedian makes jokes about mothers-in-law. Tyndale
says of women :

God hath wrought wonderful things by them because he would
not have them despised ... women have judged all Israel and
been great prophetesses and done many mighty deeds – yea and,
if stories be true, have preached since the opening of the New
Testament.

... If a woman were driven into some island where Christ was
never preached might she not there preach if she had the gift
thereto? Might she not also baptize? And why might she not by
the same reason minister the sacrament of the body and blood of
Christ and teach them how to choose officers and ministers? O
poor women, how despise you them !

This liberty is the liberty of the children of God :

Of God therefore we be bold as of a most loving and merciful
father above all the mercy of fathers. And of our Saviour Jesus
Christ as of a thing that is our own and more our own than our
own skins : and a thing that is so soft and gentle that, we lade
him never so much with our sins, he cannot be angry nor cast
them off his back so we repent and amend. But Master More
hath another doctrine to drive us from God and to make us
tremble and be afraid of him.

And so to Christian solidarity :

In Christ there is neither French nor English; but the Frenchman is the Englishman's own self and the English the Frenchman's own self. In Christ there is neither father nor mother, neither master nor servant, neither husband nor wife, neither king nor subject . . . but the father is the son's self and the son the father's self and the king is the subject's self . . . and so forth : I am thou thyself and thou art I myself and can be of no nearer kin. We are all sons of God, all Christ's servants bought with his blood.

Of Tyndale's writings, the *Answere unto Sir Thomas Mores dialoge* and *The Obedience of a Christian man*, which carries forward Luther's views on earthly authority and of vocation, are the most effective, and I suspect the best bits came from his sermons. He has a way of patching in paragraphs from Luther or from Zwingli but giving them an English context and his own stress. His *The practyse of Prelates* is an historical scamper through the seamy side of English Church history, not nearly as impressive or as well done as Wycliffe's similar polemic. He did best to stick to the Bible. He translated the Pentateuch and may have got well beyond it when he died. Soon for Tyndale, as for More, the shadows began to lengthen. Stephen Vaughan succeeded in getting an interview with Tyndale outside Antwerp and hinted that there might be a royal pardon :

> I perceived the man to be exceedingly altered and to take the same very near his heart in such wise that the water stood in his eyes . . . and he answered, 'If it would stand with the King's most gracious pleasure to grant only a bare text of scripture to be put forth among his people . . . I shall immediately promise to write no more . . . but immediately repair into his realm and there submit myself . . . offering my body to suffer what pain and torture his Grace will.'

If Tyndale's polemic is harsher than More's it is because he and his comrades experienced the other side of what went on in the investigation of heresy : a dark world of spies and betrayals, of prolonged examination, of torture, of the apparatus of law rigged always against the defendant who might never see his accusers or speak in his own defence. Tyndale was betrayed in the Low Countries by a renegade Englishman, himself a man of straw. He was imprisoned by the Imperial authorities outside

Brussels and eventually tried by a commission delegated from the Inquisition. From this period one letter has survived:

> I beg your lordship ... to send me from the goods he has, a warmer cap: for I suffer greatly from cold in the head and am afflicted by a perpetual catarrh which is much increased in this cell; a warmer coat also for this which I have is very thin; a piece of cloth, too, to patch my leggings – my overcoat is worn out, my shirts also are worn out ... I ask to be allowed a lamp in the evenings – it is wearisome sitting alone in the dark. But most of all I beg ... the Hebrew Bible, Hebrew grammar and Hebrew dictionary, that I may pass the time in that study ... but if any other decision has been taken concerning me, to be carried out before winter, I will be patient....

Alone, in that dark hole, like Browning's Grammarian,

> So, with the throttling hands of death at strife,
> Ground he at grammar; ...

His period of imprisonment and that of Thomas More overlapped. But for this lonely man there was no Meg Roper. Both More and Tyndale were granted rather Gilbertian privileges – More, though guilty of treason, to be executed with the axe – Tyndale, though guilty of heresy, to be strangled and then burned. Tyndale, after imprisonment for 1 year and 135 days, suffered in the early days of October 1536 at Vilvoorde, outside Brussels. Whether his last words were 'Lord, open the King of England's eyes' or no, events were already in train to give the English nation a Bible into which the best of Tyndale was incorporate.

Modern essays by Fr Tavard, by Dr Heiko Oberman and by Dr Ellen Flesseman-Van Leer have suggested that More and Tyndale represent two sides of late medieval thinking about the relation of Scripture and Tradition. More's view of Scripture has been recently examined by Heinz Holeczek in a volume *Humanistische Bibelphilologie als Reformproblem*, a book which succeeds in shedding some light on Sir Thomas More and an almost equal amount of darkness on William Tyndale. We must not press the antithesis too far. More loved the Scriptures and the best part of his poignant *Dialogue of comfort against tribulation*, which he wrote in the Tower, is an exposition of the 91st Psalm. Tyndale's hermeneutic is interesting and complex, but it is neither individualist nor subjective, and he too takes account of the common creed of Christendom. More did not die for the doctrine of the Papal plenitude of power, about which he held views which were less orthodox than he thought. For him the Papal authority was bound up with a hardly less important doctrine, that of the common sense of the faithful :

> I will advise you ... to stand to the common well-known belief of the common known Catholic Church of all Christian people, such faith as by yourself and your fathers and grandfathers you have known to be believed.

– words which to a lawyer are more precise than to us and which joined him not only with Erasmus, but with John Henry Newman of a later day.

More suggested that men would be better occupied than reading heretics' books, or even his own, if they would turn to 'such English books as may most nourish and increase devotion' – and he named the *Imitation of Christ*; Tyndale, we may be sure, would have turned wayfaring men to the reading of the New Testament. Today we should not pitch Tradition and Scripture over against one another. In the last days we have commemorated the death of another English subject in a prison, outside Brussels : Edith Cavell, who in the last weeks of her life read and re-read the *Imitation of Christ* and her New Testament. In October 1945 in a sad house in Berlin I watched Dietrich Bonhoeffer's mother hand to Bishop Bell the little book from which at the last he had made his devotions; for he too turned to the *Imitation of Christ* and the New Testament.

In Dante's *Paradiso* he makes those who were enemies on earth be reconciled in heaven, and so St Thomas Aquinas, as a kind of heavenly praelector leads forward his old theological enemy, Siger of Brahant. Sir Thomas More at his trial hoped that he and his judges might one day meet merrily in heaven, together. So may we think of Thomas More and William Tyndale : men of influence indeed, by their lives and by their death.

> From such ground springs that which forever renews the earth
> Though it is forever denied.

5

John Knox: The Voice of the Trumpet*

> He cannot stand still at the voice of the trumpet.
> When the trumpet sounds, he says 'Aha!'
> He smells the battle from afar,
> The thunder of the captains and the shouting.
>
> Job 39:24

JOB'S DESCRIPTION of a war horse is magnificent, but Lord Alanbrooke said it is an even better picture of Winston Churchill. And better still of John Knox, who belongs inescapably to Christ's Church Militant. We do not much like military metaphors nowadays, but his writings are full of them, and 'trumpet' is his word, almost to the point of obsession. And at least the word makes us sit up, for it is very evident that in our modern ecumenical orchestration, among its sounding brass and tinkling cymbals, trumpets are in short supply.

Had he chosen a text it might surely have been 'Give God the glory: as for this man we know that he is a sinner'. And those who have written most perceptively about him, Lord Eustace Percy and Pierre Janton for example, tell us to begin with the inward man, with Knox's prayers. He knew the heights and depths which lie behind the phrase 'Justification by faith alone', which not only Luther but Gerard Manley Hopkins have so poignantly described:

> O the mind, mind has mountains; cliffs of fall
> Frightful, sheer, no-man-fathomed. Hold them cheap
> May who ne'er hung there.

I know [said Knox] how hard the battle is. . . . I know the anger, wrath and indignation against God calling all his promises in

---

* A Sermon preached in the Kirk of St Giles, Edinburgh, on 26 November 1972, in commemoration of the Fourth Centenary of the death of John Knox

doubt and being ready every hour utterly to fall from God ...
against which rests only Faith ... wherein our most desperate
calamities shall turn to gladness and to a prosperous end.

And then he was not only a Paul man but a John man,
joining Romans and Galatians with St John's Gospel, and
Ephesians. There, in the seventeenth chapter of St John's Gospel,
the colloquy between the Eternal Son and the Eternal Father is
where his soul last cast its anchor, but he rested there many
times, from his first call to preach, huddled with his bairns in
St Andrew's Castle, in the galleys pondering Henry Balnaves's
astonishing treatise, at the heart of his treatise on Predestination,
and in the Scots Confession at the point of eucharist – 'ut ipsi in
Christo maneant et Christus in eis'.

In Van Eyck's great altar piece, there are two side panels. On
one side the young warriors, in their vigour and prime, with
banners, armour, swords, and the great war horse pawing the
ground. On the other, the old men, hermits and pilgrims leaning
on their staves. John Knox begins in the one, clasping his great
two-handed sword as chaplain to George Wishart. And he ends
an old bent man, leaning on his stick – 'miles emeritus' – but the
clue to both is that they are turned to the vision of the Lamb.
John 17 : Master Calvin's sermons on Ephesians; and Isaiah 53.
These were the famous last words which he read.

His prayers, and then his preaching. 'Send out preachers',
wrote Calvin to the Duke of Somerset, 'whose trumpet voices
will reach into the corners of men's hearts.' It is with the great,
small company of Edwardine preachers that he really belongs :
with Latimer who denounced great sinners by name in the
presence of a King; with Bradford who like Knox called on
whole cities to repent; with John Foxe who was not only a
prophet but a seer and who discerned the shape of things to come.

Like Luther, he took Ezekiel 33 with deep seriousness. He was
God's watchman, called to sound an alarm, as one who must give
an account, at whose hand blood might be required. It is the
clue we must admit to some of Luther's most unhappy writing
against the Jews, and some savage pages in Knox's *Admonition*.
But we have never touched the vocation of preaching unless we
have known what it is to be bound with a whole people, not only
in a solidarity of suffering, but also in a solidarity of guilt, such

as today binds the Reformers to us, and to the Protestants in
Northern Ireland.

Knox had for apostasy a medieval revulsion against a lapsed
heretic. He knew the primitive Christian polarity between the
traitor and the martyr. England had heard the gospel, had begun
its reformation, as after 1560 had Scotland. And he believed
nations do not get two chances.

> The sun keepeth his ordinary course and starteth not back from
> the West to the South : but when it goes down we lack light of
> the same until it rise the next day . . . so it is with the light of the
> gospel, which has its day appointed wherein it shines to realms
> and nations : if it be condemned, darkness follows.

It is this which accounts for the fierce bitterness of his last
days. He would not have enjoyed the hymn 'Eyn' feste Burg'
for it would have reminded him of the 'damnable house of the
Castle of Edinburgh', and its two inmates, the Laird of Grange
and Maitland of Lethington, on whom he turned a fiercer wrath
than ever directed against the two Marys – for these were once
his comrades, might have been the Mr Standfast and Mr Valiant
for Truth of the Scottish Reformation, turned into Mr Facing
Both Ways and Mr By Ends.

We are most restive at Knox's little dooms and judgments,
the univocal relation he finds between the Old Testament and
his own day, the ever-repeated Ahabs, Jezebels and Jehus, re-
clothed in kilts and kirtles and bonnets, begging, it seems to us,
all the questions of which since Vatican II we are all aware. But
amid so much that is naïve and simplistic, we had better heed
Knox's words :

> My assurances are not the marvels of Merlin, nor yet the dark
> sentences of profane prophets, but the plain truth of God's Word,
> the invincible justice of the everlasting God.

The historian Froude said :

> One lesson and one only history may be said to repeat with
> distinctness, that in the long run it is well with the good, that in
> the long run it is well with the wicked.

Knox would have queried 'long run' and we in fear and

trembling, and remembering Auschwitz and Dresden may wonder if we have reckoned with the prophetic interpretation of history. And when we smile at those geographical expostulations, which in Gilbey and Bradford come so near to bathos, 'O Bolton, repent! Turn to God, O Manchester! O Scotland! O England, England!', have we in our gospel reckoned with the sins of cities and of nations, on the nexus between manners and morals and that Righteousness by which the nations stand and fall? With the shattering truth that I belong to Glasgow, but Glasgow belongs to God?

He had a knack of turning up, of steering for the sound of the guns, in him a bit of an adolescent David who in the naughtiness of his heart, had come to see the battle. But when he came, the news, 'John Knox is come', made Papists hastily bring meetings to a close and timid Protestants stared at one another with a wild surmise, for he was like Luther in this too, that he not only scared his enemies but also terrified his friends. But his was the clear, ringing trumpet known which not once or twice rallied the ranks in the very moment of panic and despair. Thomas Randolph, that Lloyd George-like politician with a Welshman's nose for a sermon, has told us :

The voice of this one man is able in an hour to put more life in us than five hundred trumpets blustering in our ears.

If we could see John Knox – this is the X in the equation – we should understand why he and not Willock or Craig or Erskine of Dun bore the prophetic brunt of Scotland's reformation, that vibrant fire which again and again brought his accusers to awe-struck silence. Three great qualities he had. Integrity : the man was a hero to his valet **as** Bannatyne confessed :

It has pleased God to make me a servant to that man John Knox whom I serve, not so meikle in respect of worldly commodity as for that integrity and uprightness I have known.

Shakespeare saw 'tickling Commodity' – self-interest as the hall-mark of the venal age. In his will Knox said :

None have I corrupted, none have I defrauded, merchandise have I not made of the Evangel of Jesus Christ.

And courage : for in the pulpit he neither feared nor flattered any man. And when one gibed, 'You are not in the pulpit now', he had the answer :

I am in the place where I am demanded of conscience to speak the truth : therefore I speak.

And loyalty : in a time of turncoats, traitors, ever changing sides and breaking faith, Knox could say that he had never abandoned a friend or failed his country :

In your most extreme dangers I have been with you : Sanct Johnston, Cupar Muir and the Crags of Edinburgh yet recent in my heart : yea and that dark and colourous hour wherein ye all, my Lords, with shame and fear left this town, is yet in my mind.

And wherever he went, a Church grew – first those house communions in the homes of the lairds, then more and more the great audiences, and the devout companies of men and women earnest, hungry and thirsty for the Word of God. And there were his people elsewhere, his ministry in Berwick and Newcastle with its Baxter, Kidderminster-like flavour – in Dieppe in France and Frankfurt in Germany, for, as Thomas Fuller said, his merits naturalized him in any Protestant congregation and above all in Geneva with his dear flock of exiles for Christ's sake. Jean Guitton says that letters to women reduce the pain of writing, and we do not need to remember St Francis of Sales, or Fénelon or John Wesley, or even John Bradford, who is the closest parallel to this correspondence of ghostly counsel. There was that which came upon him daily : the care of his mother-in-law, but then Mrs Bowes was no black sheep, but a rather silly, woolly lamb who thought that the sins of Sodom and Gomorrah were eating peas with a knife. It is Anne Locke who was the prophetess amongst them to whom he shared his triumphs :

We do nothing but go about Jericho, blowing with trumpets as God giveth strength, hoping for victory by his power alone – Christ Jesus is preached even in Edinburgh and his blessed sacraments rightly administered in all the congregations – Edinburgh, Saint Andrews, Dundee, Sanct Johnston, Brechin, Montrose, Aire and now upon the south borders – so that the trumpet soundeth overall, blessed be God.

And so the frame of a great Church – a Confession, which however composite its authorship, bears his mark upon it. And a liturgy and a discipline. The art of the possible did not include its educational vision, but the devout imaginations of John Knox won through in the end. His Scotland produced more school-masters and doctors to the square mile than any country in Europe. I was not surprised some months ago in the deep south of New Zealand, within touch of the cold winds from the Antarctic, to find a community built by Scotsmen, with a fine University, and to see that the finest theological library in the southern hemisphere was in Knox College, Dunedin. And are not the roots of this in Knox and his vision of the commonalty of Scotland?

> Neither would I that ye should esteem the Reformation and care of religion less to appertain to you because ye are not kings, rulers, judges, nobles or in authority. Beloved brethren, ye are God's creatures, created and formed to his own image and similitude, for whose redemption was shed the most precious blood of the Son of God.

John Knox was not the very model of a modern ecumenical. But in his controversy with the Jesuit there is one splendid hint of better things to come :

> We are bold to affirm that if it ever shall please Almighty God to bring the Kirk of Rome to her original purity, she shall not be ashamed to embrace and reverence the Pure Kirk of Scotland as her dearest sister, and next resembling her in all things – she shall vote in our favours, against all such as shall deny us to be a Kirk.

Vatican III, who knows?

But if that prophecy is unfulfilled, we are here today to fulfil another. About old man Knox there is a touch of King Lear. It was the ingratitude which hurt :

> What I have been to my country albeit this unthankful age will not know, yet the ages to come will be compelled to bear witness to the truth.

It might have comforted his old heart to know that four hundred years after we should come from north and south and east and west to do him honour as a great servant to God, from Churches where the trumpet of the gospel is muted or even forced to be silent, and perhaps from Churches only too given to blowing their own trumpet, yet knowing that if we had not come, the very stones of this place would cry out. This noble church has been called the heart of Scotland. While he spoke within it it was also a great nation's conscience.

> One who never turned his back but marched breast forward,
>   Never doubted clouds would break,
> Never dreamed, though right were worsted, wrong would triumph,
>   Held we fall to rise, are baffled to fight better,
>   Sleep to wake.

So he passed over, and all the trumpets sounded for him on the other side.

6

Matthew Parker, a Man*

WHAT IS USUALLY called 'The Elizabethan Settlement'
might better be called 'The Elizabethan Unsettlement', for the
story is full of holes. There are gaps in the evidence – during
those first fateful months after the accession of Elizabeth, and
again during the 'brabbling' period of 1565–6. And the religion
of the Queen herself? If, as Bacon said, she did not like 'to make
window's into men's hearts and secret thoughts', she kept the
blinds well drawn over her own. There has been every temptation
for historians to rush in with their own wild surmises. Nor is it
easy to avoid reading back into those years notions of later date –
Protestant, Catholic, Puritan. The two dire moments of identity
crisis for the Church of England, the periods 1640–60 and 1830–
60, have made the business of labels so desperate that at least two
historians – R. W. Dixon and F. W. Maitland, no less – were
driven to invent their own vocabulary: 'Romanensians',
'Augustans'. Others in this fourth centenary year have spoken of
Matthew Parker's contribution to the religion and thought and
history of the Church of England. I shall only attempt a plain
account of Matthew Parker the man.

He was born at Norwich, 6 August 1504, and all his days he
was grateful ('he himself has said it and it's greatly to his credit')
to be a Norfolk man. It was among Norfolk men that he found
his University friends – Thomas Bilney and Robert Barnes, and
in the Lollards Pit outside Norwich that he watched Bilney
burned to death. During Ket's rebellion he preached a courageous
sermon to the rebels from the 'Reformation Oak' on Mousehold
Heath. It was from Norfolk that he took his wife, and a set of
alms-houses near Norwich was his best commemoration of her.
If the care of all the churches came upon him there is no doubt

* A Lecture given in the Mill Lane Lecture Rooms, Cambridge, on 4
March 1975, during the Quatercentenary Celebrations of Archbishop
Matthew Parker (1504–1575)

from his correspondence that those of the diocese of Norwich had for him particular interest and concern.

A note among his manuscripts records the exact day (though not the right year, 1520) when he came up to Cambridge, on the Feast of the Nativity of the Virgin, 8 September. He became a Bible Clerk at Corpus Christi College in 1521 and a Fellow in 1527. He was made Deacon and ordained Priest in that same year, and he took the higher degrees of B.D. in 1535 and D.D. in 1538.

He was a friend of the leading trio of Cambridge Reformers, Bilney, Barnes and Latimer, and perhaps closest to Latimer. Like them, he knew the writings of More and Erasmus, and turned eagerly to the new critical tool of the Erasmus New Testament. But these men were not simply 'Erasmians', and the famous White Horse Inn opposite Corpus which they thronged was nicknamed 'Little Germany', not 'Little Rotterdam'. We do not know how many Parker read of those 'banned books' of the 1520s – the strangely eclectic lists of commentaries and Common Places, of Luther, Melanchthon, Zwingli, Lambert of Avignon – but we do know that similar Biblical commentaries by Luther, Musculus, Calvin, Beza, Bullinger were among those of the next generation whose volumes he left at the end of his life to the University. When Parker was summoned from Cambridge to attend on the Queen Anne Boleyn as chaplain, it was to serve a lady who treasured her beautiful copy of Tyndale's New Testament, who was perhaps the most convinced adherent of the Royal Supremacy, and a partisan of the new Biblical theology, and a doughty opponent of the tyrannies of the Bishop of Rome.

Some months later Anne made him Dean of the College of Stoke-by-Clare, and it was not long before he became involved in controversy with Dr Stokes, his senior in years and academic standing. The words he wrote then were true for him forty years on :

> There can be no better service to God than sincerely to declare his will and pleasure, no sacrifice more acceptable than to con-vert the hearts of his reasonable creatures in true faith and knowledge unto him, and no ways better can we deserve of the commonwealth, than by our diligence to continue the commons in a quiet subjection and obedience toward their governors, and to further love and peace among themselves.[1]

And he goes over to the attack :

> Peradventure some there be that will be glad and desire to hear you allow their old trade, and superstition, and papistical dregs.[2]

> I trust in God's grace I shall bear all personal injuries and slanders well in worth, as hitherto I have done...but if the injury or slander redoundeth to the word of God, to the majesty of that, or to the decay of my prince's authority and lawful ordinances, or to the disturbance or commotion of the commons, I will never for friendship suffer that, but will do my uttermost to revenge it.[3]

It was at his little college of Stoke that he first displayed his quite uncommon flair for administration, his care for learning, and his love of building.

His draft of new statutes for this medieval foundation was taken as a model by the Duke of Norfolk : he was to show equal talent in making other statutes for his college, for the University of Cambridge, and for hospitals at Canterbury. His new arrangement for lectures on the Bible by visiting scholars, four days a week, part in Latin and part in English, which the clergy must attend, is in line with the best fifteenth-century practice; it is also the heart of that which began in Zürich in 1522 and was to become known as the 'godly exercise' of prophesying. He took delight in building, as he was later to do at Canterbury and Bekesbourne, at Corpus Christi College, and in that notable gift to the University, the road which he laid down between Great St Mary's and the Schools. His gifts were always imaginative and humane. For he remembered what it was like to be a student squelching through the mud with poor shoes, to shiver in the cold (he provided money for a good fire in his college), and to be lonely. We have the testimony of one of the Stoke boys, Thomas Bowsley, of how Parker kept an eye on him at Corpus, and took him on trips to Norwich and to Ely. When Parker endowed his bursaries at Corpus he ensured that the boys should be provided with the tools of learning, their Erasmus Greek Testaments and dictionaries of the sacred languages.[4]

After the suppression of Stoke – deferred out of respect for the splendid, if small-scale, achievement of its Master – it was to Cambridge that he turned. In 1544 he became Master of Corpus Christi College, and in a few months he was everywhere and

everything : doing the office of a bursar, straightening the
accounts and making the first real inventory of property, re-
writing the rules for the loan chest – the famous 'Billingford
Hutch' – arranging the Library, rebuilding the Master's Lodge,
and devoting the moneys saved to scholarships, where Norfolk
boys had priorities. Early the following year he was made Vice-
Chancellor by a wide margin of votes – with Nicholas Ridley a
very bad second. That at his re-election in 1548 there were no
dissentient votes is due to his services to the University in the
intervening years, when the possessions of the University came
under envious scrutiny : Parker headed a pre-emptive delegation
to the King, and it was Parker's own meticulous roll of Corpus
accounts which so impressed the King that for the University the
day was saved. As Vice-Chancellor he had to manage a difficult
relationship with the Chancellor, Bishop Stephen Gardiner. There
is an acid comment on Gardiner, which comes to life among the
scissors-and-paste stuff of Parker's history of the British Church,[5]
to the effect that Gardiner had been one of Wolsey's young men,
and had been infected from him with lust of pomp and power.
Gardiner could hardly find congenial the Parker who in that
Indian summer of English humanism warmed to its two marvels
of learning, John Cheke and Thomas Smith.

But Gardiner could not forgive the University for taking to
Cheke's views on the right pronunciation of Greek, and in 1545
he began a disgruntled correspondence with Parker. It began with
sarcastic references to the problem of 'decayed cooks' in Cambridge – their small labour and smaller wages; and then began
a great row about a play performed at Christ's College, the
boisterously anti-Roman play *Pammachius*, parts of which were
highly offensive to the taste of Henrician orthodoxy. Those
of us who have writhed in embarrassment, wondering what the
young men will say next, will understand why Parker and what
Gardiner called 'the sage' of the University had counted absence
the better part of valour, but when Parker handed over the in-
sufficiently censored script Gardiner wrathfully appealed to the
Council. It was all accompanied by rather modern mutterings
about students :

If learning should now be an instrument to stir up dissension, and
trouble the common quietness, their opinion should be confirmed

74

which not many years past have laboured to prove in books printed in English that the Universities be the corruption of the realm.[6]

It ended with hints from Gardiner of wider charges – 'I hear many things to be very far out of order, both openly in the University and severally in the Colleges'[7] – and there is some doodling by Parker on the back of the letter which makes a list of things which might well be improved – as student attendance at lectures and the shaving of their beards!

He was not personally involved in the theological debates of Edward's reign. But he was intimately linked with the short but deeply influential stay in Cambridge of the Strasbourg Reformer, Martin Bucer. Bucer as a young Dominican had been won to Luther at the Heidelberg disputation in 1518: he had spent the rest of his life and energies as a Reformer, writing with his crabbed hand treatises, polemic, commentaries and a great correspondence, and attending innumerable consultations in a long eirenical attempt to bring the Swiss and Wittenberg theologians together in the great eucharistic debate; an architect of liturgical reform in two cities, Ulm and Cologne. Now old and as he said 'one-eyed', shivering in the inhospitable climate in Cambridge, this great character not only influenced disciples like the young Edmund Grindal and the late-vocationed John Bradford, but deeply impressed friends like Parker who helped arrange his lectures, got him the D.D. which qualified him as a Regius Professor of Divinity, dined him and his formidable wife, loaned him money, declaimed at his death the funeral panegyric, and acted as executor — even though it seems some of Bucer's books and papers mysteriously did not get nearer to Strasbourg that the Corpus Library.

Parker had the misfortune to fall in love at the very time when the Six Articles came down against clerical marriage, and the result was the seven-year understanding with Margaret Harlston, whom he married on Midsummer Day, 1547. About her Parker gives the best short comment:

This Margaret, my most dearly beloved and virtuous wife, lived with me some twenty-six years, and died right Christianly on the 17th of August, 1570.[8]

75

It was an exceptionally happy marriage – on which that very bachelorish bachelor Nicholas Ridley's famous question, 'Has she got a sister?', is an apt gloss. And when she died, a light went out of Matthew Parker's eyes.

It was this clerical marriage which led to Parker's deprivations from his livings in the first part of Mary's reign. Ill-health may be one reason why he did not go into exile, but into that retirement into which Archbishop Cranmer would also willingly have gone. For the rest of the reign, he lived in hiding : perhaps among friends, no doubt in Norfolk.

> After this I lived as a private individual, so happy before God in my conscience, and so far from being either ashamed or dejected, that the delightful literary leisure to which the good providence of God recalled me yielded me much greater and more solid enjoyments, than my former busy and dangerous kind of life had ever afforded me.[9]

So he turned to his books, with a wide range of humanist interest, and much solid modern divinity, and the new editions of the Fathers. He wrote a metrical version of the Psalms and, if it is not great poetry, it is a bridge between the ancient spirituality of the Catholic Church and the new reformed use of metrical Psalms. And he adapted a treatise of John Ponet about clerical marriage which had arisen in controversy with Gardiner.

There seems to have been at least one moment of danger : 'Flying in a night, from such as sought for me to my peril, I fell off my horse so dangerously, that I shall never recover it.'[10] Three effects those years seem to have had on him : they made him a permanent semi-invalid; they gave him an inward turn towards the happiness of his home; and they made him more of an antiquary and a little of a recluse.

In the first months of the new reign, Elizabeth with difficulty stood upright against the many and great dangers which beset her. That the existence of Elizabeth herself, and the survival of England, were desperately at stake, that England was spared the ruin of civil war, unlike Scotland, France and the Netherlands, to become to the Counter-Reformation the bastion, the Malta of Protestantism, is because of the dedication of the Queen and her advisers to what Parker called 'policy', even to the point of constant dissimulation (which in anger he once called 'this Machiavel Government', and which was to override all other considerations, including a consistent Church policy). But it was a Church with gaping holes in the episcopate – with the old guard dominant among the lords spiritual and in Convocation. The fiasco of the Westminster confrontation which broke down in a modern enough way, on a row about the agenda for the agenda, showed the weakness of the Marian prelates; though in those first weeks there were two very notable speeches by Archbishop Heath and Abbot Feckenham which posed both theological and practical dilemmas : the question whether Rome was a 'true' or a 'malignant' Church, and the shaping in an English accent of the grand question, 'Where was your Church before Luther?' which dominated Protestant apologetic for a generation. And when the Queen took, instead of 'Supreme Head', the title 'Supreme Governor', this did not solve all the problems about the extent and limits of spiritual jurisdiction. In his very last letter Parker put it to Cecil :

> Whatsoever the ecclesiastical prerogative is, I fear it is not so great as your pen hath given it her in the Injunction, and yet her governance is of more prerogative than the head papists would grant unto her.[11]

I think some of the Queen's often unpredictable hesitations are a witness to these uncertainties.

In those vital first months Parker was but marginally concerned: illness kept him from the key committee to devise services; he took no part in the Westminster confrontation. It was with alarm and despondency that he greeted the obvious firm intention of William Cecil and Nicholas Bacon to bring him into the centre of affairs – there have been fewer more sincere 'Nolo Episcopari's' than his. He begged Bacon that he might rather be enabled

> to occupy myself to dispense God's reverend word amongst the simple strayed sheep of God's fold, in poor destitute parishes and cures, more meet for my decayed voice, and small quality, than in theatrical and great audience ... But to tell you my heart, I had rather have such a thing as Benet College is in Cambridge ... than to dwell in the deanery of Lincoln.[12]

But he protested too much, for in outlining with great perception the qualities of a true archbishop he seemed to Bacon to outline himself :

> God grant it chanceth neither on arrogant man, neither on fainthearted man, nor on covetous man. The first shall both sit in his own light, and shall discourage his fellows to join with him in unity of doctrine, which must be their whole strength; for if any heart-burning be betwixt them, if private quarrels stirred abroad be brought home, and so shall shiver them asunder, it may chance to have that success which I fear in the conclusion will follow. The second man should be too weak to commune with the adversaries, who would be the stouter upon his pusillanimity. The third man not worth his bread, profitable for no estate in any Christian commonwealth, to serve it rightly.[13]

It seems to have been a very short, short list; Nicholas Wotton, a career diplomat; David Whitehead, an Irish Archbishop-Designate, who had turned radical in middle life and been pastor of the Frankfurt exiled congregation. The Queen knew of Parker as her mother's chaplain and if she could have remembered little of the sermons he had preached before her at the age of two and five we may suppose that Cecil and Bacon told her much about the achievements of this impressive Cambridge trouble-shooter. Parker loved to quote words which Anne Boleyn used about her daughter, a week before her arrest – it is unfortunate that none of those who heard the story has handed them down to posterity.
Parker's attitude to greatness thrust upon him was simple.

> Alas! alas! O Lord God, for what times hast thou kept me. Now am I come into deep waters, and the flood hath overwhelmed me. O Lord, I am oppressed, answer for me, and strengthen me with thy free Spirit : for I am a man, and have but a short time to live.[14]

But in the end he had to obey,

> referring yet myself wholly to your grace's pleasure, rather than by just allegiance of mine unworthiness the loyal duty of my faithful heart should be any ways suspected to your reverend Majesty.[15]

Certainly he never faltered in his duty of obedience and faithful determination to fulfil what he now accepted as his vocation.

Yet his relationship with the Queen went wrong from the start. The lawfulness and propriety of clerical marriage was for him not only an important theological doctrine but perhaps the deepest fact of his own personal life. Yet it was a thing which the Queen despised, and which from time to time angered her beyond measure. There was not only the obvious fact that married clergy had additional motives for enriching themselves and for providing for their families and therefore of augmenting incomes which she was engaged in paring to the minimum. She refused to do more than wink at a married clergy, and her refusal to give them legal status thus endangered the inheritance of their children. Her order to exclude all women from colleges and cathedral precincts caused Cox of Ely to write in panic to Parker, and finally Elizabeth poured all her wrath on Parker.

> I was in an horror to hear such words to come from her mild nature and christianly learned conscience, as she spake concerning God's holy ordinance and institution of matrimony... Her Majesty moreover talked of other manner Injunctions that shall hereafter follow. I trust God shall stay her heart.[16]

Under stress Parker had a lively prose style and he continued, privately, to Cecil:

> Horsekeepers' wives, porters', pantlers' and butlers' wives, may have their cradles going, and honest learned men expulsed with open note, who only keep the hospitality, who only be students and preachers, who only be unfeigned orators, in open prayers, for the Queen's Majesty's prosperity and continuance; where others say their back pater-nosters for her in corners... yesterday's talk... have driven me under the hatches and dulled me in all other causes, mourning only to God.[17]

There is perhaps a guardian angel of history who keeps and makes up the good stories. We may be grateful for the one which tells how at the end of her lunch with the Parkers at Lambeth the Queen said to her hostess:

> Madam I may not call you : mistress I am ashamed to call you : so I know not what to call you : but yet I thank you.

Alone of her near advisers, Parker got no nickname. He learned to listen meekly to her frequent chiding at Council and Court, as he wrote to Lady Bacon :

> This other day I was well chidden at my prince's hand; but with one ear I heard her hard words, and with the other, and in my conscience and heart, I heard God.[18]

Once at least, he answered back :

> Her highness lamented much the dulness of praying in her court, and fasting – and I added the great negligence of having God's Word last Sunday.

She who could charm ambassadors, mayors, and citizens with a gesture and a smile, had few smiles for him; though once in the middle of an angry set-to, she turned and beamed at him (fiercely whispering that it was for the sake of the crowd and of his public office). Yet he cherished each kind word and it was the great gratification of his last years when Elizabeth came to be his guest at Canterbury. He planned meticulously as only he could, down to every last detail – got all the facts he could of the great feasts of Church history, of which that of Archbishop Neville of York was the most famous – how many dishes? how many guests? – and when it was all over wrote a letter of rare and almost boyish enthusiasm to Edmund Grindal of York.

His only great confidant was Cecil : Cecil who shared so many of his own bookish tastes and antiquarian interest, the one man to whom he could let down his hair, so that about every three months there were letters in which he poured out his griefs and frustrations; he was to Cecil something of what old mother Bowes was to John Knox.

Elizabeth did not care for Bishops : she could neither flirt with them nor box their ears. They were perhaps rather a poor lot compared with her great sea captains. They were of course a second eleven, and the English Reformation story would have been very different had men like Cranmer and Ridley and Rogers and Rowland Taylor not been destroyed. It that curious frontispiece to Parker's History of the Antiquity of the British Church his own shield and coat of arms are at the centre, the shields and arms of his fellow bishops fill the rest of the page – curiously like the defending shields of Saxon knights around their king.

By the end of the 1560s they had learned to stand together but in the critical first years they went their own ways, and offered Parker their friendship but not what he most wanted, their obedience. At times he could be brutally outspoken as when he bade Bishop Sandys 'to live and leave off talking' or when he rebuked Parkhurst, who had spoken of the delicate task of distinguishing genuine from vain prophesying – 'Good my lord, be not offended; it is a pity we should shew any vanity in our obedience'. They stood under common danger of the filching of their lands, and a common impoverishment. The way in which their children intermarried is more than coincidental, and bespeaks their isolation as married bishops in the new society.

The returning exiles had not spent all their time in quarrelling, nor were they all fanatics. Even the extremist Knoxians stayed in Geneva to finish their great Geneva Bible which held first place in the hearts of Englishmen until the time of John Bunyan. The students among them heard the same teaching they had heard from Bucer at Cambridge, and in Strasbourg almost the same lectures they had heard from Peter Martyr at Oxford. They brought back grateful memories of generous hospitality and protection, above all, perhaps, towards Bullinger and the magistrates of Zürich, a pressure point along the great escape routes for Protestants between Italy and Poland, between Switzerland and England. They had seen great cities where medieval abuses had been done away, which had begun to tackle that third dimension, 'the Discipline of Christ', which the second generation of reform had added to 'Word and Sacrament'. They had seen godly companies of men and women, sitting devoutly under the Word, singing the new metrical psalms with fervour. Cities where heresy did not go unpunished, and from whence the Anabaptists had long since been expelled. If Bullinger and the theologians and magistrates of Zürich constantly supported the English policy in regard to vestments, it was because they too gave the *jus reformandi* to the godly magistrate. The English radicals like Sampson and Humphrey resembled not so much the Reformers of the Swiss cities, as those rebels, Conrad Grebel and Felix Manz, also University dons, who began the Anabaptist movement. In the first months of Parker's episcopate, one of his chaplains, John

Man, Warden of Merton College, Oxford, translated into English and dedicated to Parker the formidable *Common Places*, a thousand pages in all, of the Berne theologian Wolfgang Musculus, which included a massive section on the Civil Magistrate and his authority in matters of ceremonies. The statement of faith which the refugees made on their return to England is a document, as Dixon noted, of dignity and moderation, explicitly repudiating the doctrines of Knox and Goodman – and sought out and used by Parker as he revised the 42 Articles into the 39.

Parker was perhaps happiest in Kent: not so much at Canterbury as in his little manor house at Bekesbourne; green fields, retired, with its little trout stream. His imagination had not many distant horizons. Some rather insular historians think it meritorious that he had never, unlike his colleagues, been further abroad than the Isle of Wight. But the reason why he, not a former exile, was chosen Archbishop is surely because he had not been involved in the *émigré* quarrels, on either side, and had no mental scars, or broken friendships. Yet it was no advantage that he did not know France and Frenchmen as John Knox learned to know them in his tormenting months of labour at the galleys, or travelling dangerously to and from Geneva, or labouring anxiously among the faithful at Dieppe. If he had his children taught French, it was because he had to cope with visitors from France, notables who expected costly gifts, and misbehaved, distinguished refugees who outstayed their welcome. For Parker believed, with the famous marginal note in Aylmer's book against Knox, 'God is English'. 'Where Almighty God is so much English as he is', wrote Parker, 'should we not require his mercy with some earnestness?' In 1564 he was greatly alarmed at the ill-preparedness of Kent to receive a French invasion – hence his amusing treatment of the French ambassador:

> I walked in my garden under the sight of his eye, as talking familiarly with my neighbours the gentlemen of the country... And because they much noted the tract of this country in the fair plains and downs so nigh the sea... in a little vain brag (unpriestly ye may say) I thought good to have a piece of mine armoury in a lower chamber, nigh to my court, subject to their eyes; whereby they did see that some preparation we had against their invasion, if it had been so purposed.

Good enough for Captain Mainwaring and Dad's Army! The visitors behaved better than Parker had expected:

> I could not charge them either with word or deed, or purloining the worth of one silver spoon: somewhat otherwise than I did doubt of before.[19]

But there was no naïveté about his concern for the French Church:

> Upon hearing of a Diet for conference of learned men appointed in France [he wrote to Cecil] I wished that Mr [Peter] Martyr, or Calvin, or both, could be procured thither; they were as able to stand in defence of a truth ... as the adversaries striving against God ... We be careful to re-edify a decayed temple, which is a good deed; if we all were as careful to help the re-edifying of so great a church as France is to Christ again ... it could not but turn to our own quiet at home, to have more friends in conjunction of religion; which is of more force to bind amity durable in men's hearts, than all extern worldly policies whatsoever.[20]

And he did what he could to welcome the refugees when they began to stream over. One of the really happy days in his life was a visit to Sandwich, where the leading layman Roger Manwood (who had bought and helped to rescue Cranmer's manuscripts) was planning a grammar school:

> I this last Sunday morning rode thither from my house, and was there by seven of the clock; the rather so soon, to prevent their civility of receiving ... but ... they prevented me; for, though the morning was very foul and rainy, yet I found the mayor and his jurats ready at the town-gate to accompany me to my lodging, and so to the church ... My auditory great and attentive to hear ... The strangers there being very godly in the Sabbath-day, and busy in their work on the week-day ... I mean to commend the town's request to the Queen's favour ... to express to you some part of my joy which I have here by them in this outward corner of my diocese ...[21]

And so that day the town won Parker's heart and its new grammar school.

Articles, Injunctions, Visitations: these were the tools of episcopal discipline as they had been for centuries. The royal visitations which began the reign, Parker's own metropolitical visitations, and the visitations in each diocese, in some of which, like Bristol, Parker was involved during the vacancy of a see, soon laid bare a depressing picture of a pastorate in gravest disarray – the desperate shortage of ministers, to which the deprived Catholics and soon-to-be-deprived Puritans were to add aggravation. The old abuses of pluralism, non-residence, and decay of churches went on. The shortage of ministers drove Parker and his colleagues to desperate measures, to mass ordinations of men without learning or stability, mechanics and journeymen of a kind which might delight a modern bishop but appalled and affronted their congregations, so that that first experiment was soon retracted; hardly less successful was the device which in Scotland also had been temporarily accepted of an order of readers who could at least mutter the homilies. And at all levels, greed, corruption defied Parker's attempts to clean up his own Court of Faculties, which he would fain have abolished, and bedevilled even his own visitations – as when he found that his own minor officials were taking bribes, that others were using the visitations not to impose discipline but to make money, while the sale of ecclesiastical offices vitiated every level of administration by acts of near simony from which to his horror he found that even Nicholas Bacon was not immune. It was one thing to survey and diagnose a situation, quite another to reform. If we go back to a fifteenth-century archbishop like the great Nicholas of Cusa we can see how inadequate the machinery of visitation could be, and how things could revert once the visitor had gone away and what ecclesiastical hackles about jurisdiction bishops and deans could be relied on to raise against any metropolitan, in the sixteenth as truly as in the fourteenth century. In this, as in some other ways, Parker was the last medieval Archbishop of Canterbury.

New questions, says Newman, demand new answers, and the truth seems to be that the old methods and measures were insufficient to deal with abuses so long entrenched, and deeply rooted into the fabric of temporal as well as spiritual life. And when the new sixteenth-century problems had also to be dealt with – recusancy of Catholics, especially in the north of England, and the new ferment of Puritan agitation – then there was need of such new devices as under Whitgift were fatefully to be devised, a permanent court of High Commission and the inquisitorial method of the *ex officio* oath – efficient but ominous enough to make the ageing Burleigh remember the gentle Parker with more affection.

It is not necessary here to refer in detail to the Puritan controversy, which has been chronicled by Dr Harry Porter and Professor Patrick Collinson. It must have seemed in the first months of Parker's rule that the settlement might work, that the greater part of the Church would accept the Act of Uniformity and the Injunctions. The beginnings of the 'vestment controversy' must have seemed something which might only be a repetition of the trouble caused by Bishop Hooper in the reign of Edward. The obstinate rebel, the old arguments, the old solution : that the civil magistrate must be obeyed for conscience, sake when he makes rules for things indifferent, of ceremonial law.

But now it was not a question of the mistrust, which old Coverdale and Fox as well as Cox and Parker shared, of popish garments, and of the offendicle of the cross and the candles of the Queen's chapel, but the fear that these things were but a prelude to a general relapse of the nation into Popery. These apparently trivial things, as Sampson and Humphrey wrote to Beza, were but a rallying point for other abuses of a more sinister kind. They were symptoms of a Church where the ancient abuses of the medieval Church went on unreformed, while the growing demand for the reformation of reformation itself was attacked with all the engines of ecclesiastical sanction, with the sequestering of livings and the deprivation of clergy. Parker's attitude was clear and did not waver :

> Does your lordship think that I care either for cap, tippet, surplice, or wafer-bread, or any such? But for the laws so established I esteem them, and not more for exercise of contempt against law and authority, which I see will be the end of it.[22]

Parker accepted a hierarchical view of an ordered society where all men obeyed according to their station and vocation. 'God keep us', he wrote in 1559, 'from such visitation as Knox have attempted in Scotland : the people to be the orderers of things.' But Knox too had been horrified to read what Parker read in Sleidanus. And in 1573 Parker warned Cecil :

I fear ye shall feel Muncer's commonwealth attempted shortly. It must needs follow whereof Sleidan writeth in his history, if the law of the land be rejected, if the Queen's Majesty's injunctions, if her chapel, if her authority be so neglected, if our book of service be so abominable, and such paradoxes applauded to.[23]

This was not reactionary hysteria. Three-quarters of a century later there was such dire convulsion of Church and State in England. There was revolution. The question to be asked is whether Parker's own 'mediocrity'[24] is in fact to be identified with the *via media* as later Anglicans conceived it; and whether (though this is maybe an unfair question as it surely is if asked of Parker alone, or even of the Queen and Parker) in fact the pressures of history did not enforce a middle way so narrow and so rigidly interpreted and enforced as to make that future great catastrophe inevitable.

What one man could do Parker did valiantly, not least in those months of 1565–6 when he was left to go it alone and bear the brunt of public displeasure, and to put out his 'Advertisements' without royal authority or even the looked-for assistance of temporal counsellors. By this time he was only too aware of the soft-pedalling even of men like Cecil as he wrote about the Cambridge situation :

You ... will suffer so much authority to be borne under foot by a bragging brainless head or two ... your conscience shall never be excusable. ... We mar our religion; our circumspections so variable ... maketh cowards thus to cock over us. ... Execution, execution, execution of laws and orders must be the first and the last part of good governance; although I yet admit moderations for times, places, multitudes, &c.[25]

There came that trial experiment in London which was so easy to caricature – Mr Robert Cole standing dressed in the prescribed habits, like something out of a Wippell's catalogue, and a scared and angry Chancellor saying peremptorily, 'Ye that will presently subscribe – *Volo*, I will – so write : you that will not subscribe – *Nolo*, I will not. Be brief : make no words : so is the order : peace peace. ...' Parker noted that some of the best refused to subscribe, and showed 'reasonable quietness and modesty otherwise than I looked for'. But there were also the trouble-

makers, of little learning and judgment. And on the eve of trying
out the Advertisements on London :

> What tumult may follow, what speeches and talks be like to rise
> in the realm, and presently in the whole city ... we leave it to
> your wisdom to consider. We trust that the Queen's Majesty will
> send some honourable to join with us two, to authorize the rather
> her commandment and pleasure.[26]

In April 1566 he was tried to the limits of his own energy :

> sitting ... about brabbling matters ... this whole week ... I ...
> am compelled to keep my bed ... I can do no more, nor can
> promise any more; my age will not suffer me to peruse all the
> parishes ... My lord of London and I in our letters jointly signi-
> fied ... many speeches would arise, and much resistance would
> there be ... At my first speech with the Queen's Highness ... I
> answered, that these precise folk would offer their goods and
> bodies to prison rather than they would relent. And Her Highness
> willed me to imprison them ... Must I still do all things alone?...
> The care committed unto me only, as though the burden must
> be laid on my neck ... All other men must win honour and
> defence, and I only shame to be so vilely reported. And yet I am
> not weary ... to do service to God and to my prince; but an ox
> can draw no more than he can.[27]

And a fortnight later :

> I trust her Highness hath devised how it may be performed. I
> utterly despair therein as of myself, and therefore must sit still,
> as I have now done, alway waiting either her toleration, or else
> further aid. Mr Secretary, can it be thought, that I alone, having
> sun and moon against me, can compass this difficulty?... I shall
> not report how I am used of many men's hands. I commit all to
> God. If I die in the cause (malice so far prevailing) I shall commit
> my soul to God in a good conscience.[28]

Parker knew that there were pressures at Court to bring his (and
the Queen's) devices to nought :

> If there be not some more severity extended, and some personages
> of reputation expressing a more discontentation towards such
> disorderly doings, it will breed a cease one day in governance.

And now my lord of London ... seeth the marks and bounds of these good sprights, which, but for his tolerations &c. had been suppressed for 5 or 6 years ago.[29]

In the last years of his life, he had to endure full scale attacks upon his person, and on his life-style, as the Pope of Lambeth and of Benet College. And the malice went beyond words :

this last term, where *quidam filii Beliall* (some sons of Belial) did gouge my poor barge in divers places in the bottom, that if it had not been spied, I was like to have drenched in the midst of the Thames (no great loss, yet of such one as I am); but I would have been sorry my family to have perished.[30]

Yet he himself had little malice in him and he could take care that the poor crazy brother of Thomas Cartwright should be kindly treated, and he dealt kindly and generously with a whole succession of Catholics who were billeted on him, from Thirleby and Boxall who lived in his household for years, to a succession of recusant gentry and clergy whom the Council thought might be talked out of the great refusal.

He did not despise the Geneva Bible, and in the dearth of copies of the earlier Bibles was prepared to license it, but he persevered with his own project during the troubled years of the Elizabethan Unsettlement with his Bishop's Bible, into which he himself put a great deal of editorial work and a manful share of translation, and to which he added many of the attractive features of the Geneva Bible. His prefaces are worthy to stand beside those of Thomas Cranmer, and are an index to his own spirituality :

Search therefore, good reader ... the Holy Scripture, wherein thou mayest find thy salvation. . . . Occupy thyself therein in the whole journey of this thy worldly pilgrimage, to understand thy way how to walk rightly before him all the days of thy life. . . . Only search with an humble spirit ... seek with purity of life, knock with perpetual perseverance, and cry to that good Spirit of Christ the Comforter.[31]

Here is a kind of catholicity, words which John Gerson and Martin Luther and John Bunyan might have written.

In the last years of his life against the background of the Papal
Bull of 1570, the Plots, the treason of the Duke of Norfolk, the
turbulent Queen Mary of Scotland, he was more and more concerned by the renewing strength of Catholicism; the noble quality
of life of men like Edmund Campion; a new brilliance of
Catholic apologetic, demanding to be learnedly answered. It was
a great joy to him when John Jewel, in the midst of much tire-
some apologetic, could write a small, compassable classic, his
Apology for the Church of England, something which could be
sent to other lands, and at home read in the fine translation by
Lady Bacon.

It was the English counterpart of Luther's cry, 'We be the
true, old, Church', just as in his Paul's Cross challenge Jewel
had at last retorted to the gibes of Heath and Feckenham that
it was Rome and not the English Church which had brought in
deadly innovations. And it was here, as Sir Edwyn Hoskyns
showed in two famous College Sermons, that the significance of
the Parker Library and of the Parker manuscripts really lies.
Parker, like Cecil, was an antiquarian, a book-lover and a book-
collector. In some ways he belongs to the age of Trithemius and
Nicholas of Cusa and Pope Pius II, in his love of books and zest
for manuscripts. But it was the Protestant humanism, too, of
Flacius Illyricus and his *Magdeburg Centuries,* and Bale and
Foxe, compassing sea and land to seek out manuscripts, and he
shared Bale's lament that so much of priceless value had been
destroyed in the Reformation, and so many valuable manuscripts sold and exported, so that it was from Flacius that he got
his first extracts of Matthew Paris. He thought that to recover
Cranmer's great notable works from the shelves of Dr Nevynson
was as good work as to repair a chancel, and got Ralph Morice,
Cranmer's secretary, now retired with him at Bekesbourne, to
write down all he remembered of his master, so that the sections
on Warham and Cranmer in his *History of the Antiquity of the
British Church* (in the main a compilation of his own secretary
John Josselyn) contain highly interesting new material, and would
deserve a careful modern source criticism.

He could never get enough books, and had agents in England
and Wales as well as overseas – one of them, with the delicious
name of Batman, seems alone to have swooped on 600–700
volumes in under four years. The result was the great collection

which enriched the University and his college at his death. And he looked after a good printer like John Day, who privately printed his 'book of Antiquitie' and even more fatefully invented an Anglo-Saxon type. 'I have within my house in wages, drawers and cutters, painters, limners, writers and bookbinders.' But it was his collection of Anglo-Saxon books and manuscripts, the life of Alfred by Asser, eucharistic treatises and sermons, which made him not only a pioneer in Anglo-Saxon studies but gave a picture of religion in Britain in former ages of great worth for Protestant apologetic.

Sir Edwyn Hoskyns drew attention in a 1932 Corpus Sermon to the extraordinary care with which Parker guarded the library:[32] the Master and Fellows to take oath for its safe keeping; the three keys so that the consent of Master and two Fellows was essential for access. Apart from the Pepys Library at Magdalene, which may have copied those conditions, the only parallel I can think of is the Pentagon – the keys and the brief case and the President and the 'Bomb'. If that sounds grotesque, Parker might have said that history is the ultimate deterrent and truth the ultimate explosive. I think that is what Sir Edwyn Hoskyns meant when he said that the manuscripts of Corpus are not only a charter of English freedom but materials of vital importance for the defence of Parker's beloved Church of England.[33] He never took part in the great Westminster debates; he might have made a fool of himself had he done so : but the questions – whether worship should be in the vernacular, whether a national Church has authority to ordain rites and ceremonies; whether the sacrifice of the Mass is against Scripture – these are the very questions on which Parker's Anglo-Saxon documents bore, of a British Church, an Anglo-Saxon Church where in fact the usage was contrary to the Church of Rome and – for good measure and as a happy bonus – clerical marriage was permitted !

Like Martin Luther, like John Knox, Parker's last months were shadowed by fears of the coming age, and with reason. He lost his wife in 1570, and with her his best reason for living. He was almost constantly ill, he had perhaps as many enemies as friends at court, including the vicious hostility of Leicester. He knew the times were against him :

We must reform such things as most part of gentlemen be

against ... But if this be not looked unto, I will plainly give over to strive against the stream.[34]

In that fine last letter, he charged Cecil to

help her Majesty's good government in princely constancy, whatsoever the policy of the world, yea, the mere world, would induce. To dance in a net in this world is but mere vanity. To make the governance only policy is mere vanity.... But I cease, and refer all things to God.... I am compelled thus to write, lying in my bed, by another man's pen.[35]

I think there may well be truth in Strype's story that on his death-bed Parker dictated a bitter letter to the Queen complaining not about his enemies but his friends – about William Cecil and Nicholas Bacon for their failure to prevent the spoiling of the Church, that 'patrimony of Christ' and of his poor – a fact which Whitgift too speedily communicated to Cecil.

So died this wise, courageous and gentle man. To speak of him, with Frere, as steering the Church of England to safety is to claim more than can even be claimed for Captain Elizabeth and master mariner Cecil. Perhaps John Jewel had the right word when he wrote to Parker in June 1563 : 'Your Grace is *sacra anchora* (a holy anchor) unto me and others.[36] He was the anchor man. The anchor to a Church caught in a gale off a lee shore, compassed with swift and deadly currents which might have dragged her to disaster. He loved to quote old Latimer's saying about a bishop being a watchman, and this too he had faithfully been. I think he would not have claimed as much. He would have written about himself those words which he put in the margin of Sir John Cheke's pathetic recantation, 'Homines sumus' – we are men, after all.

The idea that it is the function of an Archbishop to 'give a lead' to the Church seems to me a modern notion : it receives little encouragement from church history, which records that the few who have tried to do so, Thomas Becket, Archbishop Sudbury, Thomas Cranmer, William Laud, have come to a frustrated and sticky end. Only one person in Parker's England could 'give a lead' – the Supreme Governor herself. That to which Parker was committed and by which he is to be judged, lay in another dimension.

Are you ready, with all faithful diligence, to banish and drive away all erroneous and strange doctrine contrary to God's Word?

Will you shew yourself gentle, and be merciful for Christ's sake to poor and needy people, and to all strangers destitute of help?

Will you deny all ungodliness and worldly lusts, and live soberly, righteously, and godly, in this present world . . . that the adversary may be ashamed, having nothing to say against you?

The record is that he was so ready, that he did indeed so shew himself, and we are grateful for his good example.

7

William Bedell, 1571–1642*

WILLIAM BEDELL[1] was baptized in the parish church
in the village of Black Notley, in the County of Essex, on 14
January 1572. It seems to have been a potent font, for some
years later another Black Notley baby, John Ray,[2] was dipped in
its water. Bedell's father was a yeoman farmer, comfortably off.
Ray was the son of the village blacksmith. But as young William
trudged to school in nearby Braintree, he passed herbs and wild
flowers to which, one day, the great naturalist John Ray would
give a local habitation and a name. Two Cambridge worthies are
glory enough for a little village.

William's schooldays left their mark on him in a rather special
sense, for a clout on the ear from an angry usher sent him spin-
ning down a flight of stairs, leaving him permanently deaf in one
ear, so that his aversion from music in church may have the non-
theological cause, that he had only one ear for music. But he was
bright enough to be sent in 1584 to Cambridge at the age of
twelve, to be one of the first batch of scholars at the new foundation of Emmanuel, under its first Master, Laurence Chaderton.
From him Bedell learned something which seems to have slipped
from our curriculum, what he calls 'the art of dutiful obedience'.

He became the favourite pupil of the great moral theologian
William Perkins, of Christ's, and on his teacher's death bought
his library. He also began his long friendship with Samuel Ward,
one day to be Master of Sidney Sussex College, Lady Margaret
Professor of Divinity, and a British representative at the Synod of
Dort. We may call these men Puritans. But Bedell was to protest
in a sermon before the Bishop of Norwich that 'he wished the
names of Puritans and Precisians might be cast to hell, that we
might be known by the name of Christians'. At any rate
Emmanuel's Puritanism was by now of the sober kind, leaving

* A Commemorative Lecture given in the Old Library, Emmanuel
College, Cambridge, on 1 December 1971

93

revolutionary Presbyterianism to the dons of Trinity, and 'surplice brabbling' to St John's. Chaderton himself was so little inclined to make point of conscience about vestments or a parity of ministers that his main contribution to the Hampton Court Conference which he attended in 1604 was eloquent silence, while Ward refused to take the Covenant, and was put in prison for siding with the King. It is true that they were Calvinists, and that Bedell and Ward thought that Arminianism was not only wrong but poisonous, and while Bedell was always lending around his copy of Calvin's *Institutes*, he had no copy of Hooker. But like most of his friends he quotes Melanchthon, Chemnitz and Beza more often than Calvin. There is a page in the Lambeth MS of Chaderton where half a page of quotations from Beza is followed by half a page entitled 'Thomas', meaning St Thomas Aquinas. Bedell can quote Gerson and the nominalist dialectic of the ordained and absolute power of God, as well as Bellarmine and the Jesuits, and of course Augustine and the Fathers – all this learning giving priority to the study of the Bible, using the best linguistic tools.

Bedell received a very thorough classical training, and achieved a spoken and written Latinity of Ciceronian elegance, while he wrote a fair Renaissance hand. He was also grounded in Hebrew, Arabic and Syriac. In the course of his seventeen years in Emmanuel College he took his degrees (B.A., 1588; M.A., 1592; D.D., 1599) and became Fellow, Catechist and Bursar of the college. Emmanuel was rather proud of one of its statutes which forbade a member to remain a Fellow on attaining the degree of Doctor of Divinity – not primarily on the ground that any D.D. resident in Cambridge must needs be an academic layabout, a plausible argument not in fact mentioned, but simply because the object of the college was to send men out into the pastoral ministry. So Bedell was priested by the Bishop of Colchester and in 1602 left to become incumbent of the Church of St Mary, Bury St Edmunds.

East Anglia was then a place of excitement for the young clergy. Today, like the Elizabethan Government, we can make too much of the Puritan attempt to establish a presbyterian system within the Church of England, and the conflict about vestments, and subscription. But there was at this time a genuine attempt to bring together in brotherhood the ministers, gathering in sodalities like the famous Dedham Classis, and meeting regularly as they did in Bury, for sermons followed by conference and dinner at which clergy and leading laymen joined together.[3] Bedell shared in such associations, but for him the controverted matters of vestments and subscription were not the point of conscience, since he believed that the continuance of a Christian ministry and the preaching of the gospel had priority. He held with the first Elizabethan Reformers, with Foxe and Coverdale and Jewel, that these other things were indifferent matters where the godly magistrate might rule. And he quoted in support the great continentals, Melanchthon, Bullinger, Beza, brushing aside the arguments of those who said 'Yes, but these were strangers and saw not our estate' with the crushing retort: 'As if they composed these doctrines concerning ceremonies or indifferent things as prognosticators do their Almanacks, for their own Meridian only'.[4] He became a noted preacher in the plain style, which kept the apparatus of learning in the study, and many came a long way to hear him. But the church was roomy and he had a weak voice so that St Mary's became rather a strain. He married the widow of the Recorder of Bury, who brought with her four children by her first marriage, to which they added four of their own, two dying in infancy.

But however we rate Bedell's Puritanism, there is no doubt about his sturdy Protestantism. Throughout his lifetime Catholicism continued to gain ground while both sides increasingly appealed to violence. He shared the national euphoria at the discovery of Gunpowder Plot, and every year afterwards on 5 November he expounded Psalm 124 – 'If the Lord had not been on our side . . .' – and read out a letter which had been sent him from London during the fateful hours of 5 November 1605. The idea that it was all a plot cooked up by Robert Cecil to discredit a promising liberation Movement, and that today Guy Fawkes and his friends would deserve a grant from the World Council of Churches, would not have appealed to Bedell – or to me. But at any rate the plot caused Bedell to burst into poetry. About this he wrote rather solemnly to Ward :

Touching Poetry, I doubt not but it may be used by a Minister in a holy sort. Gregory Nazianzen, Apollinarius . . . and many others are example, even in Ministers.[5]

Very much as Victorian parsons turned to Robert Browning, so Bedell's circle admired Spenser and so Bedell's *Shepherd's Tale of the Pouder-Plott*[6] affects the style of Spenser. Colin Clout reappears, and his grumpy old companion Thenot, and two new characters – Willy and Perkin (shades of William Perkins!) Alas, it is only fit for An Anthology of Bad Verse, slightly above the radical poet Samuel Bamford's 'Ode to his dying Dog' and McGonagall's 'Tay Bridge'. You may find the following lines curious – and modern :

> Theire Powder they brought into the same place
> By little and little secretly,
> And there dispose it thriftily,
> In Baggs and Barrels; save that one great Tunn,
> Right under the Chaire of State they done.
> They would be sure the King should be sped,
> All were but lost, but if he were dead;...
> This Guilty Vault is with Powder freight,
> Above Three Thousand Six Hundred weight;
> Enough (they say) to blow up a Town,
> And rase with the dint half a Country down.

It did not get into print until 1713 and was a worst seller. At this time, too, Bedell wrote a spirited reply to William Alabaster (whom he keeps calling Mr Alablaster, which it must be admitted has a more satisfying ring for debate), the neo-Latin poet who had defected to Rome; and though his friends thought it worth publishing, it remained in MS until Alabaster had returned to the Church of England in the 1630s, when Bedell refused to publish, despite pressure from Ward and Archbishop Ussher.

Then, out of the blue, came an invitation to go as Chaplain to the Embassy in Venice. There were three such chaplaincies vacant and they all went to Emmanuel men, as Izaak Walton said, 'bred in the same University, all of one College, all beneficed in the same Diocese, all most dear and entire friends'.[7] The friendship became rather strained when the first of the trio, James Wadsworth, went to Madrid, and immediately became a Catholic, and soon was tutor to Henrietta Maria. The other was Joseph Hall, and it is notable that while Sir Edmund Bacon had nominated Bedell for Venice, he chose Hall to go as his own travelling companion, to France. For Hall was the coming man, brilliant preacher, satirist, wit, sure to go right to the top. Bedell had learned too well Master Perkins's *Direction for the Government of the Tongue* and too often refrained even from good words. But perhaps Bacon was perceptive. Venice at that moment offered, it seemed, a fleeting but tremendous opportunity of being won over to the Protestant cause. Like other cities, Zürich for example, it had in the later Middle Ages more and more asserted its right to control the Church and clergy and had established a lay suzerainty which came easily into conflict with post-Tridentine clericalism and papalism under Pope Paul V. The resultant struggle over benefit of clergy brought the great republic under an Interdict, and though it had come to an end, more by the intervention of Henry IV of France than from a lot of fussing from James I, before Bedell's advent, relations were still strained between the two powers, and it seemed, at any rate to our Ambassador Sir Henry Wotton, that Venice might be induced to ally itself with a Protestant League.

Soon Hall was writing to Bedell : 'We have heard, how full of trouble and danger the Alps were to you', and he continued flamboyantly :

If you know it not, the Church, our Mother, looks for much at your hands : she notes your graces, your opportunities, your employments : she thinks you are gone so far, like a good merchant, for no small gain; and looks that you shall come home, well laded.[8]

So Bedell came to the splendid city and he may have thought that earth had not anything to show more fair – save Cambridge. It was a Venice nearer to the Venice of Ruskin and Turner than the raddled old Madam of our day, all light and sunshine and blue water, palaces and piazzas, gardens and gallant walks – giving no outward sign that already her glories were fading, her titles soon to vanish, her strength to decay.

Sir Henry Wotton was a colourful character, as Izaak Walton's nice sketch and Pearsall Smith's[9] well documented *Life* abundantly show. Handsome and dashing, he had all the gifts of a diplomat and he revelled in the cloak-and-dagger stuff. There was the occasion when James I was at Stirling, and an Italian visitor was announced as Ottavio Baldi – and the King listened with amazement as the visitor immediately harangued him in Italian with vast gestures, each of which brought him a step nearer to the king, in whose ears he was at last able to whisper : 'Only Henry Wotton, you Majesty! May I have a word in private?'

His wit was celebrated. One evening in an Italian church a priest slipped him a note. On it were the words : 'Where was your Church before Luther?' John Jewel had considered this a leading question and had written at length upon it, while even Bedell wrote a memorandum. But Wotton at once scribbled a retort : 'Where your Church never was. In the word of God written'. Wotton much wanted to write a life of Luther, but never got round to it, and the only contemporary English biography was by another diplomat, Sir Thomas Roe.

Then in 1604, in Augsburg, his wit nearly cost him his career, for he had written in a Visitors' book his marvellous definition of an Ambassador : 'An Ambassador is an honest man who is sent to lie abroad for the good of his country'. It lay thus for years until spotted by a Catholic publicist who printed it as evidence of perfidious Albion, and it infuriated James. Wotton kept a motley gang of bully boys whom he called his 'good fellows'. These secret agents lay in wait and intercepted the letters of what he called 'these prowling Fathers, the Jesuits'. At this time when many young gentlemen visited Italy with their tutors there was a policy of putting the tutors in prison, so that the young men could be brain-washed, and here Wotton played the role of Scarlet Pimpernel with the papal nuncio as Citizen Chauvelin.[10]

The British Embassy was full of young men, and Bedell's Emmanuel capacity for playing bowls stood him in good stead. He gave them supervisions in classics, and read them edifying books and conducted divine service in English within the embassy. But Bedell was soon caught up into Wotton's great ploy. The most important man in Venice was its official theological consultant in the fight with Rome, the Servite Paolo Sarpi, a scholar of great eminence, and a man of parts who shared with Bedell a love of plants and gardening. He and Bedell took to one another at once and became great friends, though as a leader Bedell thought him too Melanchthonian, when a Luther was called for. The papal nuncio and his agents did all they could to thwart Wotton, and he did not dare be seen with Sarpi. But Bedell was told off to give weekly lessons in English to Sarpi and his colleague Fulgentius, while Sarpi helped Bedell with his Italian and his Hebrew. Then came the attempted assassination of Sarpi, who was stabbed repeatedly and left seriously wounded by two clerics who scampered off into diplomatic and papal immunity.[11] But he soon recovered and the lessons were resumed, and Bedell would wait in the *Golden Ship* in the Merceria, until the clank! clank! clank! of dagger-proof armour announced its arrival, with Sarpi safely tucked away inside it. The plot thickened. Bedell began to preach in Latin and Italian to clandestine audiences of Venetians. Two enormous crates of books arrived from England, driving the papal nuncio frantic with rage as he tried to divert them from Customs into the hands of the Inquisition, while Wotton claimed them for the diplomatic bag.[12]

Though the nuncio was unable to prevent the free distribution of large numbers of copies of Jewel's *Apology*, Powell on Anti-Christ, and the most relevant of those inevitable Problems of Mr Perkins, the *Problema de Romanae Fidei Ementito Catholicismo*, he may have been cheered to think that the gesture revealed a certain innocence of the Venetian mind which might in the end be counter-productive. When Wotton presented a beautifully bound copy of King James's latest theological treatise, with a brilliant speech, the Doge whispered amid the bowings and the courtesies that the book was to be hidden away and locked up.[13] Bedell hopefully translated the Prayer Book into Italian and found an ally in John Diodati, the Genevan Reformer whom Wotton had invited to Venice as the man who had translated the Bible into Italian. Finally, because he thought the Venetians needed education in a sounder political tradition, and as an antidote to Machiavelli, Bedell, in those last days of a genuine theological common market, translated into Italian Sir Edwyn Sandys's book *Europae Speculum*. Then, like a mist, the whole project dissolved. Probably the English were babes in the wood of Italian diplomacy, and mistook an ancient anti-clericalism for sympathy with Protestantism. But it is true that Sarpi and his friends stood within a North Italian evangelical tradition which modern research is revealing, and both Bedell and Sarpi knew themselves at one in what they regarded as the few essentials of the faith.

Bedell went back to his books. He translated into Latin Sarpi's *History of the Interdict* and the last part of his *History of the Council of Trent*, promising to take back the manuscripts to England where they might safely be published.[14] Sarpi's *History of the Council of Trent* is a monument in Renaissance historiography, and is still required reading in Section III of Part III of our Theological Tripos. It gives a grimly critical account of the failure of the Council to achieve far-reaching reform, and sets the weight of clerical vested interest against a long historical perspective. There is a good modern assessment of it in William J. Bouwsma's *Venice and the Defense of Republican Liberty*.[15] Sarpi's history must have impressed Bedell with the difficulties as well as the need for reform of abuses which still lingered in England, which had not even achieved a Council. He went back, too, to Hebrew studies at the feet of his beloved master the Rabbi Leo and bought the lovely manuscript of the Hebrew Bible which may still be seen in our library. Nobody perhaps can stand on the quay at Venice without hearing the breeze whispering 'Come East, young man' – and before returning to England Bedell made a trip to Constantinople, about which we could bear to know more.

Then back to Bury he went, bearing his sheaves with him, paper sheaves alas, with nothing to show for the attempt to convert Venice but one convert, Dr Jasper Despotine, who settled down to an affluent medical practice near Bury and became Bedell's most intimate friend, the one to whom even more than to Ward he would confide.

Bedell went back uncomplainingly to the echoing pulpit of St Mary's and there he stayed until that great lay patron of Puritans, Sir Thomas Jermyn, presented him to the living of what looks like Horningsheath but which I am told must be pronounced Horringer. Let us not underestimate the importance in his life of those seventeen years of pastoral care. They were probably the happiest of his life. All that remains are the firm, clear notes in the parish register of baptisms, weddings and funerals. But his ministry could be taken as a living commentary on George Herbert's *Country Parson* or Richard Baxter's *Reformed Pastor*. He was diligent in preaching and in catechizing and in visiting, but he rated even above these things bringing forgiveness to wounded hearts, and the reconciling of estranged people with one another. 'This', he wrote to another minister, 'is the worthiest and principallest part of your commission, which the Apostle calls the *Ministry of Reconciliation*.'[16] And Cambridge was not far away, so that he found time to read and exchange memoranda, for the Emmanuel Puritans were great memoranda men, while extremists on both sides of a growing divide were dashing into printed volumes.

But as regards the great world, Bedell seemed to have become an ecclesiastical drop-out. When John Diodati came to London he could find no cleric who even knew his name. Cheapside in that age had a touch of the Piazza Navona about it, a broad place in which to stroll and where all one's friends must turn up sooner or later, and there one morning Diodati bumped into Bedell and carried him off in triumph to my Lord of Durham, Bishop Morton. Through Morton and Ward, Bedell became known to James Ussher, the new Primate of Ireland, and in March 1627 Bedell wrote to Ward that he had been invited to become Provost of Trinity College, Dublin :

> The answer that I made was this, That I was married, and had 3 children, a good seat in wholesome air, with a little parish within the compass of my weak voice; and above 100 l a year living – my wife not desirous to change – yet if I should see clearly it was the will of God I should go.[17]

Sir Henry Wotton, perhaps a little guiltily, wrote a handsome tribute to his 'singular erudition and piety',[18] while Archbishop Abbot of Canterbury wrote to the Fellows of 'Mr Beedle' as

> a man of great worth and one who hath spent some time in the parts beyond the seas, and so cometh unto you better experienced than an ordinary person.[19]

But Bedell found tensions and oppositions among the Fellows, and an alarming indefiniteness about the terms of his appointment and the extent of his powers which Ussher's pragmatism did not reassure. He retired to England convinced that he was too weak a character for what was needed. This at last brought everyone to their senses and Bedell returned to Dublin, riding out next day to meet the assembled Fellows who promised him their loyalty.[20] He made an admirable new set of statutes, using

their former ordinances, the statutes of Cambridge, and of
Emmanuel College, not forgetting the one about resident D.D.s.
He so improved things that King Charles wrote that by his 'care
and good government there hath been wrought great reformation
to our singular contentment'.[21] Then on 16 April 1629 the King
wrote to Lord Falkland requiring him to nominate William
Bedell to the bishoprics of Kilmore and Ardagh in Northern
Ireland. He was consecrated on 13 September and remained in
Ireland until his death. In 1633 Edmund Spenser's *View of the
Present State of Ireland* was published in Dublin and if Bedell
read it, as surely he must, he would have seen that what Spenser
said about the ill state of the Church of Ireland amid a Catholic
population was still terribly pertinent, and entirely accorded with
his own programme of reform.[22]

Already, in England, Bedell had become involved in what he
wryly called 'my law business'. He had startled his bishop by
refusing what he considered to be simoniacal fees on admission
to his benefice. He had taken to law a leading layman who had
filched some glebe land and thought for years that he had got
away with it. From his own experience of the brotherhood of
godly preachers he had imbibed, not presbyterian notions of
parity, but the sense of the need of a bishop to associate himself
with his brethren, and to consult them. And he brought to these
considerations all he had learned from his studies of the Primitive
Church. He hated pluralism with a very perfect hatred, and did
not rest until he himself had shed the diocese of Ardagh. He
continued to attack pluralism in livings, especially when it
involved imposing alien clergy who knew no Irish. Moreover,
he had perceived how the good intentions of the hierarchy could
be defeated by their own courts and officers, by greed and
chicanery and grasping at fees. Here Archbishop Ussher felt that
Bedell's reproaches must in some sense reflect on himself, for
discipline was not his strong point, and the tension between them
has been finely drawn by Dr Buick Knox in his judicious and
balanced study of Ussher. Bedell came up against his own lay
Chancellor, Mr Allen Cooke, and demanded to see his commission, which he found to be defective, and about which he don-
nishly commented to Ward :

I found a vast heap of authority conferred upon him, without

due form, Latin or common sense. One period before the
'*Habendum*', consisting of above 540 words, and yet without...
principal verb at all.[23]

When Cooke began a series of appeals which culminated in a
Royal Commission which fined Bedell a hundred pounds, Bedell
acted like an Ambrose or an Augustine :

> I went about my diocese myself, and sat in my own courts redress-
> ing the disorders, and mitigating the Fees (whereof yet I took no
> penny).[24]

The result of all this was a fury of complaint, which one correspondent summarized to Ussher :

> He [Bedell] was a papist, an Arminian, an equivocator, politician,
> and traveller into Italy.[25]

But Ward wrote to Ussher :

> I know not how my lord of Kilmore doth sort with the Irish...
> he hath godly and pious intentions : he is discreet and wise, in-
> dustrious and diligent, and of great sufficiency many ways. I do
> persuade myself, the more your lordship doth know him, the more
> your lordship will love him.[26]

The trouble with Bedell was that he not only read the history of
the Early Church but took it seriously. So he proceeded to call
his brethren together in a Synod, dining with them rather than
with the local magnate, and enacting Canons, harmless enough,
like the one enjoining burials in the churchyard rather than in
church, but, his critics said, bringing him within range of a
charge of *Praemunire*. He rode out the storm, but was soon in
such disfavour with the Lord Deputy, Wentworth, that he kept
away from him.

For by now Bedell was acting contrary to the whole government policy towards Ireland and Irish culture. Without thinking
of him as a Bishop of Rum-ti-Foo we remember that he was
entering as a missionary in a colonial situation. Bishops like
Bramhall from England, and even the Irishman James Ussher,
supported the English policy of Anglicization, and driving out the

Irish language. But Bedell knew how much was at stake. In the
Lambeth Library there is a copy of a letter from Bedell to
Despotine, who had sent him a tract he had written about the
Jesuit missions to China. Bedell detested the power politics of
the order, and had written an ironic commentary on a copy of
the Rules which had turned up in Padua. But he never un-
churched the Church of Rome and he seems to have sensed that
the great Chinese enterprise of Francis Xavier, Valignano and
Matteo Ricci was a turning point in missionary strategy, the end
of the old *tabula rasa* way of destroying an indigenous culture,
but rather a new appreciation of it which would not quench the
smoking flax but raise it to a flame. Bedell, in this remarkable
letter, approves the new strategy, and ends by wondering whether
God may not intend to provoke Europe to jealousy.[27] He himself
at any rate trod the more excellent way. As at Trinity he had
encouraged the study of Irish, so he set himself to learn the language and to teach it to his family. Every day at one o'clock the
bell rang for an Irish service in the Cathedral. He wrote a
Primer in Irish and English which he put into circulation. He
resumed an old project for an Irish Bible which had not got
beyond the New Testament, presiding over his team and bringing
to the text all his linguistic skill. And with this went friendly
contact with the Irish Catholic clergy and care for the too many
Irish poor, and constant journeyings among the Irish people.
And when disaster came, and the great rebellion broke out in the
autumn of 1641, Bedell stayed at his post, almost the only
Englishman to do so, as he was almost the only one to remain
unmolested. Of course, his house, his church and churchyard
became a haven for refugees. One night he was called to the door
to behold two dirty, dishevelled fugitives whom he did not at
first recognize as the widow of his predecessor, and one of his
own ministers – but when he did he burst into tears, and took
them in his arms, bringing to them in a few moments all the
clothes he had in the world for covering.

He might have stayed unharmed had he been willing to
abandon those who had fled to him. But when he refused to do
so he and his sons were taken to the grim castle in Loughoughter
which appears with Pre-Raphaelite tranquillity in our chapel
window : a dilapidated, damp and evil castle of Giant Despair
where only Bedell seemed to keep cheerful, a mixture of Hopeful,

Valiant-for-Truth, and Greatheart as against his sons, Mr Despondency and Master Much Afraid. After Christmas they were allowed to join the women of their family under house arrest with Denis Sheridan, an Irish minister who was able to rescue a few papers and the precious Hebrew Bible. But the Bishop was an ageing man and when deadly fever invaded the neighbourhood he too succumbed to what was probably typhus. As what was called his 'change' drew near he blessed his sons, and though pious biographers are always to be mistrusted about last words, it is plausible and in character that

on a sudden looking up even when death was already in his eyes, he spake unto them thus : 'Be of good cheer, whether we live or die we are the Lord's'.

You will have seen that Bedell was what I would call 'one George Bell of a Bishop' and not least in his care for Protestant refugees and for Christian unity. We do not know when he became a friend of that strange genius Samuel Hartlib, but Professor Turnbull thinks it probable that in his five years in Cambridge, 1621–5, Hartlib was associated with Emmanuel College.[28] Hartlib's mass of papers are full of the most extraordinary projects and inventions : for blowing up warships at one blow, for cooling rooms by means of cold water pipes (thereby inventing central heating in reverse), for using power engines to plant crops, and what are delicately referred to as 'experiments in manure and engines of motion'.

In the little Prussian town of Elbing, Hartlib had met an odd group of friends. They planned a Utopian colony called Altilia, where they thought Poles and Germans might live peacefully together, on an island in the Baltic perhaps, or even in Virginia. But Hartlib was no crackpot nor were two others of the Elbing group. For one was the great Czech educationist Comenius, whose writings Hartlib sent to Bedell, the other the Scot, John Dury, who has some claim to be regarded as the founding father of the modern Ecumenical Movement.

At the terrible climax of the Thirty Years War which brought Protestantism in Europe to the verge of destruction, Dury compassed sea and land to re-unite Lutherans and Calvinists. It came to a head in the fateful year of 1632 when Calvinists and

Lutheran divines met in a summit conference at Leipzig, and Dury invited preparatory memoranda from divines in France, England and Ireland. There is some evidence that the most important of these documents was from Bedell, for Dury used it again and again, and published it among his own papers. When a group of refugee Lutherans came to Dublin they refused the English communion service and brought themselves in danger from the law. It was Bedell who was called in and talked them into believing that there was no essential difference between Cranmer and Luther, in this matter. Nor was Bedell content with good advice. Each year he sent ten or twenty pounds to Hartlib towards Dury's vast expenses of travel and correspondence. But when in 1640 dire events took place in Britain, Bedell wrote to Ward :

> The business in Scotland hath I do believe put an end to Mr Dury's negotiation for peace. Since wheresoever he comes, it may be said to him, *Medice cura teipsum*.[29]

Bedell is said to have had a trunk of unpublished manuscripts. They included not only the defence against Alabaster, but learned and intricate memoranda on efficacious grace – which even today would make a good starter to anybody wanting to read the debate between Karl Barth and Hans Küng, about baptism, where he took a minimal view of infant baptism, about the eucharist, where though detesting the Mass, he accepted a high doctrine of eucharistic sacrifice. He did publish his letters to James Wadsworth,[30] learned and eirenical and in great contrast to those of Joseph Hall. Izaak Walton said a little glowingly that it seemed to be 'controversie who should answer with most love and meekness', which, he said, too seldom falls out in a book war.[31] Bedell himself accepted the distinction between the essentials of the Faith, which he thought were included in the Apostles' Creed, and the large area where opinions might well differ. In this he anticipates the teaching if not of his Emmanuel pupils, at least of his pupils' pupils, the Cambridge Platonists – a new eirenical temper more widely discernible than we might suppose, since it was shared by Hartlib and Dury and their friends, Chillingworth, Lord Falkland and the Tew circle, and Forbes and the 'Aberdeen doctors', in the next years.

A proof of Bedell's scholarship is the deference which Ussher paid to his textual emendations and perceptions, as when Bedell spotted that the 'Rythm of St Colombanus' was in fact a prayer. There was a splendid moment when Bedell appeared in the Court of High Commission, which he detested, to deliver solemn judgment on the unfortunate Bishop of Killala who was supposed to have praised the Covenanters and of whom Wentworth had resolved to make exemplary punishment. It was all cut and dried, and one by one the members of the court went through the motions and deplored the Bishop. But Bedell had just discovered in the College library at Trinity a copy of the canons of the first Council of Constantinople, where in Canon 6 it was forbidden to bring a bishop before a secular court. Lord Wentworth was not amused.

His hobby was gardening, and he liked to do a bit of digging every day. But he had the Emmanuel taste for planting and grafting trees, in which he was an expert.

> Good Sir [he wrote to Ward] let me entreat you to remember me to Mr Chaderton ... if he will bestow upon me 2 or 3 of his white mulberry trees, I pray appoint this bearer to fetch them, cutting off their heads. I would entreat you also to get me some grafts out of Emmanuel Coll. orchard of the timely cherries.[32]

Outside his Cathedral in Kilmore he planted a fine avenue of sycamore trees which were there a century later when John Wesley turned aside to seek out his simple grave.

He was quiet and peaceable. But he could be roused. For one thing he was a Prayer Book man and he could not abide those who either took away or added to what was by law established. When a visiting curate began to add little bits on his own, Bedell rushed down on him, snatching the book from his hands and saying: 'Be suspended from your office till you learn to read the prayers better' – and taking on from there, finished the service himself. He greatly resented the Visitation by the Archbishop because it suspended his own jurisdiction for a year, and when the apparitor-general handed him the writ of prohibition on one occasion he threw it down on the floor and stamped on it. But for the most part he lived Mr Perkins on the Government of the Tongue.

He acted as his own domestic chaplain. On rising he rang the little bell for family prayers (he kept the canonical hours, but there were family prayers thrice a day). He would translate the Psalms direct from the Hebrew and his son would reply antiphonally in Latin. He said grace himself and always read and expounded a portion of scripture at table. He kept strict account of time and money and like eminent Puritans and John Wesley kept a journal for this purpose.

Stubbornness can be a vice, but in some men it is a virtue and with Bedell it was almost a charisma. He had a quiet persistence in pursuing what he believed to be the right course which is moving and impressive. We know little of his inner life, but there is a letter to his sister in 1640 in which he says :

The prosperity or flourishing of the soul doth not stand in comfortable feeling. Either these be the flowers, yea the fruit of the spirit or I must say, plainly, farewell my part.

Tall, stooping, bearded, shy, but with an endearing smile and a wry, donnish humour, many would have agreed with Ward that to know him was to love him.

Somebody asked me the other day, 'Does this Bedell really deserve a fourth centenary celebration?' Well, you might have queried the propriety of a first, or a second, or a third centenary; but surely not this one, when before our eyes there is unfolding history's own grim memorial of the fourth centenary of the Tudor Settlement of Ireland. For some of us, one set of memories will linger all our days – those funerals, the Catholics of the I.R.A. marching beside their comrades, and firing their salute; and often in the same news bulletin, the English soldiers or the Ulster police, paying their last tribute.

There is an epilogue to the Bedell story. As his English and Irish Protestant friends bore his coffin to the grave, they were met by an armed band of Catholic Irish who did not molest them but silently divided into two files alongside the coffin. Too stunned and too frightened to take in the gesture, they did not dare to read from Bedell's beloved Prayer Book. But the sharp command rang out and the Irish raised their muskets and fired the last salute crying, 'Requiescat in pace, ultimus Anglorum'.

When Queen Elizabeth, who had not read Mr Perkins on the

Government of the Tongue and if she had would have despised it, roared at Sir Walter Mildmay, 'So, sir, you have founded a Puritan College', he replied 'No, Madam, but I have set an acorn which, when it becomes an oak, God alone knows what will be the fruit thereof', and in the statutes of the college he continued the metaphor – 'that from this seed ground the English Church might have pastors which is a thing necessary above all others'. 'For this', said Bedell, 'is the worthiest and principallest thing . . . what the Apostle calls the *Ministry of Reconciliation.*'

Worth celebrating? It is always time to mark the end of the just man. God spares whole cities for his sake.

8

Son to Samuel:
John Wesley, Church of England Man*

'JOHN WESLEY was not a man to be forgotten', said Alexander Knox, after a lifetime of reflection on the significance of the great friend and hero of his youth. And so, after two hundred years, say all of us: some of us who are Methodist Preachers, as in private duty bound, to praise famous men and our Father who begat us; all of us from a sense that John Wesley belongs to the whole Catholic Church and indeed to all mankind, concerned to appraise him against the background of critical theological and historical scholarship in which the great new edition of Wesley's Works will take its place.

Most of what needs to be said has been said and written many times and there are no great areas left wholly unexplored, save perhaps, as Professor Semmel's recent ingenious essay seems to indicate, less discussion of the origins than of the impact of the Revival on the late eighteenth and early nineteenth century. All I can try to do is to offer one or two programme footnotes to the discussion, concerned rather with the roots than the fruits of the Evangelical Revival. All historiography is selective, but conscious selectivity is perhaps a great betrayal. Nevertheless I shall venture to select one or two points where Wesley himself seems to offer a corrective to our present age, even though 'swimming against the tide' has long been abandoned from our Covenant Service and to concentrate on certain continuities between John Wesley and the Christian tradition into which he was born and bred, and which he made his own, as a Church of England Man.[1]

The century 1550–1660, or perhaps that between the Massacre of St Bartholomew (1572) and the Revocation of the Edict of

* A Paper given at Drew University, New Jersey, U.S.A., in October 1974, at a Symposium to celebrate the inauguration of the Oxford Edition of John Wesley's Works and here printed by permission of the University.

Nantes (1685), might be labelled 'the Age of Zeal' and John Wesley's sermon 'on Zeal' might in our time be published as 'A Word to a Militant'.

> Nothing has done more disservice to religion, or more mischief to mankind than a sort of zeal which has for several ages prevailed ... pride, ambition, or revenge have in all parts of the world slain their thousands : but zeal its tens of thousands.[2]

He points to the dire effects of the appeal to Violence of the so-called Wars of Religion; he deplores the hardly less disastrous violence of the tongue – religious bigotry, intolerance, the overvaluing of 'opinions' in the interests of a zeal which has outrun compassion. He even takes Hooper and Ridley to task for initiating the great 'surplice brabble' :

> Oh shame to man ! I would as soon have disputed about a straw or a barley-corn.[3]

Such intransigences left a terrible legacy and bred a vehement reaction : in Britain, the exclusion of the Nonconformists, and within the Church of England a division into parties which has bedevilled all its later history; the rejection by the Church of England of re-union with the Methodists in 1969 had its roots in the seventeenth century before Methodism was, in the petrifying of the Catholic and Evangelical wings of the Church of England, through the violence of 1640–60. In Northern Ireland there is a still more terrifying memorial of the age of zeal : where the curse of Cromwell has outlived his prayers. In the English nation there was reaction : against austerity, a permissive society, selfish and callous, a moral inflation where the weakest went to the wall. Reaction against emotion and enthusiasm : the split of the wholeness of the faith into disparate and often opposing strands of rationalism, moralism and mysticism. Yet in one field, that of Christian spirituality, there was throughout this age a wonderful flowering, blossoms and fruit of the seed sown in the first works of the Protestant and Catholic Reformation, in the great Lutheran hymns, the Psalms and 'liturgies of the galleys' and of the Desert in the Reformed Church in France, the complex treasury of Puritan and Caroline devotion in England and Scotland with, in Catholic Spain, Portugal, Italy and France, a succession of saints and missionaries and heroic sodalities unmatched by any period of Christian history. It was into this rich and many-sided inheritance of 'inward religion' that Susanna and Samuel Wesley bred their children.[4]

I in no way dispute what has been said and written of the importance, or the influence, of the incomparable Susanna, the mother of us all, on her children, nor, in the main, what has been written of her relation to the Puritan tradition. Still less would I deny what Dr Monk and Dr John Newton have said about Puritan influences on John Wesley, or Professor Horton Davies has said about the affinities between early Methodism and Nonconformist worship. But after all Susanna was the extreme High Church member of the family, the Non-Juror. So much attention has been paid to the luggage they took with them as almost to forget the destination! When at the age of thirteen Susanna, a rebel teenager, turned her back on her father's Dissent and joined the Church of England, she joined a party which rapidly became a sect. Those letters of Susanna to Lady Yarborough which turned up in the 1950s remind us of a whole side of the Wesley family life of which we know almost nothing. Susanna speaks there of seeking the advice of one of 'our divines' meaning Non-Jurors, and these letters suggest a pattern of High Church-womanship of which we could bear to know more. At any rate the Non-Juring associations were continued in some of the positive stresses of the Holy Club: the search for Primitive Christianity; the concern for frequent, nay, constant communion, for the fasts and festivals of the Church – these were more important traits than ephemeral and anachronistic notions of passive obedience, of divine right, and of loyalty to the Stuart cause, for the sake of which Susanna provoked and endured the famous family row.

When Samuel Wesley left the Dissenting Academy in Stoke Newington and trudged his penniless way to Oxford, he turned his back on the militant dissent now represented among the young men by the epigoni of the 'Calves Head Clubs' to become a thorough Church of England man, in the mid-stream of its life: as a Convocation man, as a polemic divine, as theological correspondent of the coffee-house Athenian Society, in his constant reading of English divinity and in his massive philological, biblical and patristic study. It was from his example that the

Wesley children, three boys and at least two of the girls, took to writing poetry.

It is obvious that Susanna was left to bear the brunt of their education : Samuel Wesley, gadding off for unconscionable intervals to London, leaving his wife to cope with the problems of decent poverty amid incessant pregnancies, was in line with the male chauvinism of that age; John Worthington behaved no better with his wife before him, while John Byrom did not even return to Manchester when his baby died. But let us not underestimate Samuel Wesley's part, though it is less well documented and has been far less sympathetically written. Amid all the muddle of his financial troubles, and indeed one aggravation of them, was his determination to give his sons the best education that could be got, at Westminster, Charterhouse, and Christ Church, Oxford. Susanna and Samuel were perhaps a little jealous of one another : he of her closeness to the boys and her evidently superior powers of communication, she of his overwhelming and often overbearing learning. There are signs that Samuel tried to muscle in on her correspondence with the boys, though letters were mostly shared among the family. But his own letters to Samuel junior have very good sense – and it was he who insisted that his sons should keep diaries. It was Samuel who first discovered the 'surprising thoughts of M. Pascal', and when a young lady at Oxford turned John Wesley's attention to the *Imitation of Christ* that seminal document of early Methodism, it was Samuel who broke in with perhaps wiser comments than Susanna and with the reminder that the little classic had long been his own 'old companion and friend'.[5]

Samuel it was who spoke of religious societies and of the precedent of Little Gidding; Samuel who introduced them to M. de Renty who haunts John Wesley through the years, tapping on his mind like a family ghost, an entirely sanctified Old Jeffry. It was Samuel who intercepted members of the Holy Club, journeying northwards, with the offer of facilities for frequent communion; it was his treatise on Baptism on which John was to lean heavily in later years. He drew them to Bible study based on the sacred languages. It is easy enough to caricature Samuel Wesley; the papers of the Athenian Society at their worst have too much in common with the papers of the Pickwick Club. Wherever John got his business instinct – and he thought his flair for his economy was the one talent it was death to hide – it was not from his father. But the courage to look a mob in the eye is a trait which his father learned in grim conflict with the Upland men when they destroyed his property, maimed his animals and menaced his person. And then, that fine letter of Samuel about the doings of the Holy Club – the 'Valde Probo' – there were not many country parsons who would not have deplored such eccentricities, which might ruin hopes of preferment. It is a little enough point to notice that John Wesley always signs his letters to his mother 'Your dutiful Son', and on the one occasion when he adds 'and affectionate' it moved his mother to ironical comment; yet he always signs letters to his father 'Your dutiful and affectionate son'.

For if John withstood his angry father to his face in the sad affair of his sister Hetty, the matter ended in tears and embraces from the old man and a gruff 'I always knew John was sound at bottom' – and there is no possible mistaking the pride and joy with which he acclaimed his son as Fellow of Lincoln. It was Samuel Wesley, the failed poet, Samuel the failed expositor, Samuel the failed man of learning, Samuel the failed missionary, whose ambitions were fulfilled in John and Charles Wesley. It was Samuel who, if they had known it, gave them on his death-bed the final clue in their spiritual treasure hunt : 'The inward witness – the inward witness'.

I do not wish to underrate the importance of emotion in Wesley's life, or in that of the Revival. The religion of the heart spoke to the condition of the arid emotional desert of the age as in our time the charismatic and Jesus movements fulfil an emotional need which the older Churches have not met. Yet in our age, this volcanic, apocalyptic, seventeenth-century-like world, where on all sides irrationalism seems to triumph, not least in the Church; where men are beset by problems they cannot diagnose, let alone solve; where it is not a question of controlling the present but the past which is alive – it is surely not enough for the Church simply to add yet another element of irrationality. The John Wesley we need much to hear is the author of an appeal to 'Men of Reason and Religion'. The starting point has to be Samuel Wesley's 'Advice to a young Clergyman'[6] – that astonishing document which deserves a place in the new Wesley edition. Its massive prospectus of theological learning and pastoral care would seem to be impossibly demanding, were there not evidence that Samuel himself mastered it and John too, as a comparison with John's 'Address to the Clergy' (1756) and the titles of his *Christian Library* reveal. The ground base of it all is the study of the Bible and therefore of the sacred languages, and ancillary semitic tongues. But there is a whole range of auxiliary disciplines which many of his contemporaries and of ours would have disparaged as profane learning :

> Logic, history, law, pharmacy, natural and experimental philosophy, chronology, geography, the mathematics, even poetry, music or any other parts of learning.[7]

The first three and a half years of a curate's life were to be spent in the spare-time reading of scores of volumes of biblical and patristic studies. The patristic studies of Wesley's day were not so much the devotional '*lectio*' *divina,* with which not only the Caroline divines but the great Puritans like Preston and Bolton read their Augustine, their Chrysostom, their Bernard, as that historical appeal to the authority of the Fathers and Councils which underlay the great Church of England battles against Popery and Deism, and the new critical questions about authenticity in the learned investigations of Wake and Bull and Grabe, and the studies of Tillemont and Dupin. (It is sad that Samuel and John Wesley knew so little of Augustine.)

The second three years of a curate's study were to be spent in the study of the moderns, of that great succession of English divines in the Established Church and in Dissent, whose writings Wesley described as the standing glory of the Church of England. Samuel Wesley lists their names, sonorous as a battle roll, and each with some aphoristic comment attached :

> Isaac Barrow – strong, masculine and noble.

> Cave's Primitive Christianity etc. – good books for a Clergyman's family.

And on Tillotson, perhaps over-valued by the age of Parson Woodforde but much underrated in our day :

> Archbishop Tillotson [might be said to have] brought the art of

preaching near perfection : had there been as much life as there is of politeness and generally of cool, clear, close reasoning and convincing argument.[8]

It is a vast programme of learning which would make a modern theological student swoon and even a modern theological professor turn pale. But Samuel calmly concludes :

I do not think all these books absolutely necessary, however this general view may do you no harm and ... you may read what you please and leave the rest to cobwebs.[9]

Well, there were no cobwebs on John Wesley, and whatever the young curate, Mr Hoole, made of them, his successor, John Wesley, explored them for the remainder of his life. This may be seen in Wesley's own programme of theological reading in his 'Address to the Clergy'.[10] It affronted and angered William Law who denounced it

almost all of it empty babble, fitter for an old grammarian that was grown blear-eyed in mending dictionaries than for one who had tasted of the powers of the world to come.

But in it he took over from his father the list of profitable auxiliary studies :

Is not a knowledge of profane history, likewise of ancient customs, of chronology and geography, though not absolutely necessary, yet highly expedient?[11]

Logic came first in Samuel's list and it is Wesley's emphasis on it which must have angered William Law :

One (whether art or science) although now quite unfashionable, is even necessary next, and in order to the knowledge of the Scripture itself. I mean logic. For what is this, if rightly understood, but the art of good sense? of apprehending things clearly, judging truly and reasoning conclusively?

Let the candidate for orders ask himself :

Am I a tolerable master of the sciences? Have I gone through the very gate of them, logic? If not, I am not likely to go much farther, when I stumble at the threshold. Do I understand it so as to be ever the better for it?

Does it, he asks, enable us to read with profit Henry More, Isaac Newton, Malebranche and Euclid?

If I have not gone thus far, if I am such a novice still, what have I been about ever since I came from school?[12]

What, indeed? It had been ironically remarked of little John as a child that he would not attend to the most pressing necessities of nature unless he could find a reason for it. At Oxford he lectured in Logic. In 1768 we find him writing to Joseph Benson at Kingswood :

Logic you cannot crack without a tutor : I must read it to Peter and you, if we live to meet.[13]

On at least two occasions he took text books on logic and rhetoric as themes for refresher courses for his preachers.[14] In January 1788 at the age of eighty-five his diary shows him as reading Logic on four successive mornings.'[15] In his *Compendium of Logic*, which he published for the use of his preachers and for the school at Kingswood, he expressly refers to two of his sermons as built on exact logical method. They are the Sermon on the Means of Grace, against the quietists, and the Sermon on Enthusiasm, against irrationality – both attacks on a charismatic overstress of the Revival.[16]

I am not arguing 'John Wesley : Wittgenstein's spiritual ancestor', though both men sensed the fundamental mystery of words and of human communication. Dr Anscombe sums up the *Tractatus Logico-philosophicus* of Wittgenstein by saying that Wittgenstein 'saw the world looking at him with a face; logic helped to reveal the face'.[17] From the Prayer Book Wesley learned to think of the work of the Holy Spirit as always including illumination of the mind and one of its supreme gifts as a right judgment in all things.

If Wittgenstein be too fanciful a reference, there is a luminous essay by Dorothy Sayers on 'The Lost Tools of Learning' in which she shows how words and the use of them and the right ordering of them are at the fundament of culture. Wesley regarded new words and slang as a compost heap : he did not, as we do, consider them the garden. And he would have made short shrift of our contemporary immersion in jargon, not least in the ecumenical dialogue. In one of those splendid prefaces which are Wesley at his best he confesses :

> I *could* even now write . . . floridly and rhetorically . . .; but I dare not; . . . I dare no more write in a *fine style* than wear a fine coat, . . . Let who will admire the French frippery, I am still for plain, sound English.[18]

As the Ordinal bade him, Wesley drew all his studies one way, towards the Bible. 'My ground is the Bible. Yea, I am a Bible-bigot. I follow it in all things, both great and small.'[19] He read and studied as his father had taught him, and he learned from him to abridge and condense books until he could gut them as a fisherman guts fish. He was a great borrower. Many of his famous phrases, like 'the Almost Christian', are seventeenth century. But he was no mere Autolycus, and could always pull the apt quotation from Horace or Vergil, Milton, Pope or Prior from his great memory as well as from lesser breeds without the law. And he kept up his reading to the very end. It is the old Wesley who said :

> I generally travel alone in my carriage and so consequently am as retired ten hours a day as if I were in a wilderness. . . . I never spend less than three hours (frequently ten or twelve) in the day alone.

His reading of history was wide if his interpretations were quirky : too eager to back lost causes, to accept as proven the innocence of Mary Queen of Scots or the good looks of Richard III, and he had a way of reading himself back into Church history :

> I have doubted whether . . . Montanus was not one of the holiest men in the second century. Yea, I would not affirm that the arch-heretic of the fifth century [Pelagius] . . . was not one of the holiest men of that age, not excepting St Augustine . . . [who was] as full of pride, passion, bitterness, censoriousness and as foul-mouthed to all that contradicted him, as George Fox [!] himself.[20]

His *Primitive Physic*, his clinic, his innumerable bits of medical advice show how seriously he took himself as a follower of the Great Physician. His interest in, and accurate observation of his own symptoms link his *Journals* with those of David Livingstone. And he read the important treatises as they came out, the works of Dr Cheyne, Cadogan on the Gout (though he rather doubts the value of eating pickles) and that tract of Dr Wilson on the 'Circulation of the Blood' which led him to exclaim, 'What are we sure of but the Bible?' About books of travel, geography and science he intermits credulity and scepticism :

> I read Mr Huygens's *Conjectures on the Planetary World*. He surprised me. I think he clearly proves that the moon is not habitable;.... I know the earth is. Of the rest I know nothing.[21]

This was a man of parts : but if you will read his sermons and especially the second and third series you will find that these were indeed auxiliary sciences to the Bible used as Bede and Erasmus had counselled, to illuminate the study and exposition of the Word.

I would not exaggerate Wesley's rationalism. It was for thirty years something I used to argue about with my old teacher and friend, Norman Sykes, who wrote of the 'retrograde intellectual influence' of the Evangelical Revival.

> Even John Wesley, despite his academic training and scholarly attitude, was almost superstitious in his notions of the special interventions of Providence ... and in his recourse to the expedient of the *sortes liturgicae* for the determination of his problems.... The theological and literary productions of the Evangelical revival were of little importance or permanent value to the tradition of the *ecclesia docens*.[22]

No doubt Wesley's controversial writings, his two *Appeals* and the *Letters to John Smith*, and his sermon on 'The Case of Reason Impartially Considered', do not rank with the great works of Warburton, Butler and Paley, but Wesley's works were directly suited to the needs of the revival, and to the perils which beset it, as well as to the vulnerabilities of his colleagues and assistants :

Never more declaim, in that wild, loose, ranting manner against this precious gift of God. Acknowledge 'the candle of the Lord', which he hath fixed in our souls for excellent purpose.[23]

At any rate Norman Sykes's distinguished forerunner, H. M. Gwatkin, claimed that John Wesley was one of the sanest minds of the eighteenth century.

The comments by Alexander Knox on Southey's *Life of Wesley* are among the best things ever written about him, and he has an interesting comment on Wesley's mind, and his propensity for quick decision :

He had an intellectual frame of singular construction. . . . His habits of reflection bore no proportion to his quickness of apprehension; nor could he endure delay either in reasoning or in acting. From uncertain and scanty premises he rapidly formed the most confident and comprehensive conclusions, mistaking logic for philosophy in matters of theory, and appearances for realities in matters of fact and experience.

and Knox adds :

I . . . think he would have been an enthusiast if he could. He was always gratified by hearing or reading of illapses, or raptures, or supposed extraordinary manifestations, when he was assured of the moral rectitude of the party . . . but while he thus delighted in the soarings of others, he himself could not follow them in their flights : there was a firmness in his intellectual texture which would not bend to illusion.[24]

Wesley's appeal to reason was not simply the rationalism of the age of Locke. Behind it was a long tradition of the coherence and rationality of the universe passed on to us by such great schoolmen as William of Ockham, whose positive virtues are just being re-discovered. Wesley was often prone to say, what Ockham had said before him, that God does nothing through secondary causes that he cannot do directly by himself. And Wesley was a man for economy of words and notions. He would have approved of Ockham's famous 'Razor' – not to multiply entities beyond necessity. Indeed, we might almost speak of Wesley's razor, rightly dividing the word of truth. When we read the Minutes

of the first Conferences we find it there – the risk, the adventure
of truth – the poise and balance like little boys hanging out over
a precipice and seeing who can lean furthest without disaster :

Q. Have we not . . . leaned too much towards Calvinism?
A. It seems we have.
Q. Have we not also leaned towards Antinomianism?
A. We are afraid we have. . . .
Q. Does not the truth of the gospel lie very near both to
   Calvinism and Antinomianism?
A. Indeed it does; as it were, within a hair's breadth. . . .
Q. Wherein may we come to the very edge of Calvinism?[25]

Modern theologians may stagger from one lop-sidedness to
another – from transcendence to panentheism, from Scripture to
existentialism – for all the world like the White Knight in *Alice*
whose progress was a series of one-sided crashes (the theological
name is, I think, 'polarity'). But Wesley knew how to lean over
without losing his balance, and when he tumbled, as once or
twice he did, he landed on his feet.

A signal instance of Wesley's 'Razor' is the balance he kept
between 'inward religion' and mysticism, quietism and theosophy.
Of this the *Christian Library* is convincing evidence. Behind the
diversity of men and movements in this astonishing miscellany
there is a unity. With a little topping and tailing, it is true he
made them all speak one language, Scriptural Holiness, Christ,
Methodism. Some of those patterns have been analysed in recent
years. Professor Outler has drawn attention to the Apostolic,
Alexandrian and Greek Fathers; and Professor Orcibal has
shown the debt to the French : to Poiret, Antoinette Bourignon,
Fénelon, Mme Guyon; and to the Scottish mystics – much of it
mediated by the Non-Jurors. For, as a study of the journals of
John Byrom reveal, eighteenth-century England was not all indifference and unbelief. There was a vogue of interest in religion,
pockets of intense interest in manuals of devotion. How else
explain the translation into English of the complete works of
Antoinette Bourignon, and of the writings of Mme Guyon who
may be said to have devoted twelve volumes to expounding the
virtues of silence, and the repeated editions of works like Scougal's
Life of God in the soul of Man, Castañiza's *Spiritual Combat*
and the *Imitation of Christ*? Others have drawn attention to the

high proportion of Puritan authors in the *Christian Library*, though Wesley, defending himself against the charge that he had amassed an 'odd collection of mutilated writings of Dissenters of all sorts', replied :

> In the first ten volumes there is not a line from any Dissenter of any sort; and the greatest part of the other forty is extracted from Archbishop Leighton, Bishops Taylor, Patrick, Ken, Reynolds, Sanderson, and other ornaments of the Church of England.[26]

Take this comment from Alexander Knox :

> His standard of Christian virtue was pure and exalted. He formed his view in the school of the Greek Fathers and in that of their closest modern followers, the Platonic Divines of the Church of England.[27]

The *Christian Library* contains extracts from his writings of at least eight members of one college – Puritans and Platonists, all Church of England men – John Preston, William Bedell, Joseph Hall, John Worthington, Ralph Cudworth, John Smith, Nathaniel Culverwell, William Law – all members of Emmanuel College, Cambridge.

Perhaps only two Oxford Colleges, Oriel, in the nineteenth-century, and Merton, in the fourteenth were the scene of a religious crisis of such magnitude involving great Christian men. And here in the seventeenth century there was one of the great generation clashes of history, between the Cambridge Puritans and their Platonist pupils and successors. You can almost trace it through the decades – between tutors and their brighter students in the 1630s, continues in the 1640s when the young men had become Fellows, but exploding in the 1650s when those young men were becoming Heads of Houses, Masters of Colleges, Vice-Chancellors – and of it all the most convincing evidence is the set-to between Anthony Tuckney, for the older generation, and Benjamin Whichcote for the younger men.

The new generation of learned divines reacted against both Puritan rationalism and irrationalism, against over much zeal, against 'opinions'; and if returned to the theme of Christianity as a vision of God and of a way of life. But there was deep continuity too : both sets of men were prodigiously learned, both

assumed the background of the study of the Bible and of the
sacred languages; almost all were skilled Hebraists. And yet the
poison was drawn from the great argument, despite the background of angry political convulsion, because it was a conflict
within one University and one College community, where
teachers and taught kept the bond of personal affection and
respect.

None the less, it was revolution. Sermons and philosophic
treatises and disputations – the younger men put their view not
only with learning but with a prose of majesty : Peter Sterry and
Nathaniel Culverwell wrote English which can only be compared
with the music of Henry Purcell. *Ne plus ultra*. Ralph Cudworth
was a perfectionist and he died with most of his masterpieces
still unprinted, but how right was Wesley to include in the
Christian Library that oration to the House of Commons, 31
March 1647, on 'The Life of Christ the Pith and Kernel of All
Religion' which has some claim to be regarded as the finest
oration of that age. In it Cudworth directly attacks

> our bookish Christians ... [who] think ... as if religion were
> nothing but a little bookcraft, a mere paper-skill. ... He is a true
> Christian indeed, not that is only book-taught, but that is God-
> taught; ... he that hath the Spirit of Christ within him, ... Ink
> and paper can never make us Christians, can never beget a new
> nature in us, can never form Christ.[28]

And then the attack on Predestinarianism :

> We have no warrant in Scripture, to peep into those hidden rolls
> of eternity, ... to persuade ourselves that we are elected to ever-
> lasting happiness; before we see the image of God, in righteousness
> and true holiness, shaped in our hearts.[29]

It is not for nothing that Wesley concludes his own Sermon on
Reason by quoting the text which was the watchword of the Cambridge Platonists, 'The Spirit of Man is the candle of the Lord.'[30]
He would have approver the affirmation of Whichcote against
Tuckney : 'Sir, we oppose not rational to spiritual : for spiritual
is most rational.' For reason to Wesley meant not only logic and
coherence and common sense, but the mind of man illumined by
the Spirit, the eyes of the soul to see truth. Wesley's own razor

edge between doctrine and 'opinion' has a complex historical background, but it is no product of the exhausted toleration of the *politiques*, or the indifferentism of scepticism, or even the nearer influence of the 'Latitude Men'.

But there is another facet of the Platonists to which Francis Yates and D. P. Walker have latterly drawn attention.[31] They returned to Plato via the great Florentine Platonists of the sixteenth century, to Ficino and Mirandola and through them to the Orphic mysteries, the Hermetic writings, the Cabbala – edging on to a world of gnosticism, of white magic and of alchemy. And not only the Platonists, but the new men of the Royal Society like Boyle and Isaac Newton had not disentangled their science from a mystic theosophy which was attractive but partly bogus, the kind of ferment surrounding the mysterious Rosicrucians, and the speculative mysticism of Paracelsus, Weigel and Jakob Böhme.[32] If you read Heinrich Bornkamm's two sensitive essays[33] on Jakob Böhme you will understand why Böhme's writings had for men like Henry More, John Byrom and William Law the kind of attraction that Teilhard de Chardin has had in our day. But if you turn to Böhme's writings you will understand also why they shocked and horrified John Wesley[34] as going dangerously beyond the bounds of Scripture, and why he understood the menace of this kind of theosophy for the more cultivated followers of the Revival.[35]

Yet Wesley came to the very edge, within a hair's breadth of William Law, whom he never ceased to acclaim as a good and great man and whose major treatises he himself re-published in later years. Indeed it is astonishing to discover how much John Wesley had in common with men like Henry More and William Law and John Byrom. There were moments in his life when he might easily have become such as they were, what Belloc called 'a remote and ineffectual don' reading and meditating and even retiring from the hubbub of life in a college, as More did to Ragley and Law to Putney and Kingscliffe.

But John Wesley's story is not in the end about books and ideas. Henri Talon has finely said : 'Books do not copy books, but souls copy souls'. The clash of ideas for him came within the moving context of the great Revival. 'You have to fight, not against opinions, but sin,' he told his preachers. The differences between the evangelical Calvinists and Wesley's evangelical

Arminianism were not at first very important, though they became so towards the 1770s, when Wesley was attacked with great bitterness by the Calvinists who gradually withdrew from his connexion and from the link with his itinerancy.

Wesley claimed to regard this as a difference of 'opinion' (and could therefore refrain from speaking about predestinarianism when he went to Scotland) though, if that was so, he was hard put to it to justify the expulsion of John Cennick and his friends. But this was a true perception, for Arminianism and Calvinism, like Catholicism and Jansenism, were within a common seventeenth-century crisis of Augustinianism about the character, not the existence, of grace. It cannot be said that Whitefield's Calvinism made him a more effective or less effective evangelist than the Arminian Wesley – and vice versa. A few years ago I borrowed a distinction from the Catholic theologian Rondet and suggested that Evangelical Arminianism, with its joyful universal offer of salvation – 'For all, for all my Saviour died' – represented an 'optimism of grace', as against the 'pessimism of grace' of a Calvinist predestinarianism, which limited salvation to a few elect souls.[36]

But I have to admit that when Wesley represented Henry Scougal, the Scottish Episcopalian, in the *Christian Library* it was not with his beautiful little *Life of God in the Soul of Man* but with sermons which include a terrible exposition of the theme 'That there are but a small number saved', which ends with an attack on those who

> cannot imagine that Heaven should be such an empty and desolate place, and have so very few to inhabit it.[37]

Nor can we make too much of the difference between an Arminian and Calvinist view of the freedom of the human will. We need to remember the profound comment of Berdyaev that it was the Calvinists, teaching the bondage of the will, who became the creators of human liberties, and the Jesuits, with their insistence on freedom, who supported despotism.

Yet Scott Lidgett believed that there was a cheerfulness about the Arminian piety of his home and forebears which was not so evident among the Calvinists. And certainly for Alexander Knox this happiness was a grand trait of John Wesley:

His countenance, as well as conversation, expressed an habitual gaiety of heart, which nothing but conscious virtue and innocence could have bestowed. He was, in truth, the most perfect specimen of moral happiness which I ever saw.[38]

Not for nothing did the *Imitation of Christ* link the pattern of Methodism with the lay spirituality of the later Middle Ages, with an austere life-style which was a deliberate challenge to the extravagance and selfishness of the surrounding world. Plainness of speech, simplicity of dress – Wesley set the example even if he had to spoil the opening of City Road Chapel with a tirade against the elephantine bonnets in the surrounding pews. And of course he may have known in his heart that his own white hair, and the simple black fustian which he wore so neatly, made him a more comely figure than any silks and powdered wigs.

But what converted men and women were not ideas, or principles, or a bundle or synthesis of them called Evangelical Arminianism, but Christ :

Q. What sermons de we find, by experience, to be attended by the greatest blessing?

A. Such as are most close, convincing, searching, such as have most of Christ ... the most effectual way of preaching Christ is to preach him in all his offices and to declare His Law as well as His gospel, both to believers and unbelievers.[39]

I remember a service at Littlemore near Oxford commemorating John Henry Newman, and a great French Catholic groping for a word with which to summarize Newman's religion – 'If we had to have a word for it,' he said, 'we might call it – Scriptural Holiness.' Well, there is room within the Bible for many patterns of godliness, but this was where Wesley found his religion, in the combination of the doctrines of justification by faith in Romans and Galatians with the simple audacities of his beloved First Epistle of John which led him to dare to take the Collect for Purity as meaning what it says, and God as willing to fulfil here and now his promises of sanctifying grace. He did not think of holiness as some nineteenth- and twentieth-century movements have tended to do as a kind of vague Scotch mist, but with the ordered colours of an English garden, the flowers and fruits of the Spirit, each with a colour, and a shape and a name; 'Our

Doctrines', 'Our Discipline', 'Our Hymns', 'Our Literature'
became a great frame of – to use a word despised in our time –
edification, of building up a people in grace. His genius was for
adaptation and improvisation. Like Topsy, his Methodism 'just
growed'.

> He was totally incapable [says Alexander Knox] of *preconceiving*
> a scheme. That would have implied an exercise of forethought
> and politic contrivance, than which nothing could be more
> opposite to his whole mental constitution.... That he had un-
> common acuteness in fitting expedients to conjunctures is most
> certain; this, in fact, was his great talent.[40]

Like the multiplication of a simple life-cell, the pattern grew
swiftly and ever more complex :

> I said, 'If all of you will meet on Thursday evening, I will advise
> you as well as I can'. The first evening about twelve persons
> came : the next week, thirty or forty. When they were increased
> to a hundred I took down their names and places of abode. Thus
> without any plan or design [said Wesley] began the Methodist
> society in England.

Or, as he put it elsewhere, 'two young clergymen' began to travel,
'hither and thither' – from London to Bristol, and then to Newcastle, and thence to a thousand towns and villages between and
across the border of Scotland and over the sea to Ireland and the
Norman Isles and then beyond the Atlantic, and to Africa and
the Pacific and the Islands of the seas.

Wesley's England was a green and pleasant land to an extent
we can no longer conceive : the most lovely succession of open
air theatres in Christian history, the cliffs of Cornwall, the green
boscage of Devon, the skies of East Anglia, the swelling hills of
Cumberland, the mountains of Wales, the moors and dales, the
valleys of the North and West, the smooth backs of the Downs.
And as he preached in Cornwall in the Gwennap pit, with his
back to the last rays of a setting sun, in the quiet of an English
summer evening, where not a breath, not a leaf, not one of
thousands of human beings stirred, and all melted into one in the
growing darkness as they hung on the words of one who com-
mended his Saviour – how right he was ! how much more solemn

and beautiful and majestic this scene which God had wrought, than any Gothic imitation! how much less marvellous the acoustics of the new preaching boxes in Norwich or the City Road!

> Ye mountains and vales in praises abound;
> Ye hills and ye dales, continue the sound.
> Break forth into singing, ye trees of the wood,
> For Jesus is bringing lost sinners to God.

Of course, sometimes in England it rains! And so he came to the front of the curtain, in wind and rain, and storm and often snow so deep that his congregations froze to two or three, but he never stopped his pilgrim's progress: 'One here will constant be, come wind, come weather.'

And the towns: Christopher Wren's new churches, and the even newer festering mushroom slums – and Bristol and Oxford and even Manchester walled around with gardens and babbling of green fields. And the people – the tinners of Cornwall, the keelmen of Newcastle, the colliers of Kingswood and Staffordshire, the felons of Newgate, the drunkards, swearers, sabbath-breakers at Moorfields and the harlots of Drury Lane. And the mobs which he turned into companies of devout, decent people, clothed and in their right minds, sitting at the feet of Jesus, changing the morals and manners of whole communities. Not a scene to be romanticized, for it was an age of great cruelty and callousness and need, such that unimaginable horrors must have befallen the nation in the Industrial Revolution without this revival of decencies and compassion. There is a terrible passage in one of Wesley's sermons:

> That the people suffer, none can deny;... thousands of people in the west of England, throughout Cornwall in particular, in the north, and even in the midland counties, are totally unemployed.... I have seen not a few of these wretched creatures ... standing in the streets, with pale looks, hollow eyes, and meagre limbs; or creeping up and down like walking shadows. I have known families, who a few years ago lived in an easy, genteel manner, reduced to just as much raiment as they had on, and as much food as they could gather in the field. To this one or other of them repaired once a day, to pick up the turnips which the

cattle had left; which they boiled, if they could get a few sticks, or, otherwise, ate them raw.[42]

What grew under him was a great mosaic, a design of persons, a design of friendship and many, many thousands of them were known to him by face and name. He spent thousands of hours in what his diary notes as 'conversation : tea' – and the 'tea and sympathy' side of Methodism is not to be ignored – if British Methodism had a coat of arms a cup of tea rampant would certainly have to appear on it. And there were his friends, the thousands of men and women who opened their homes and fed and boarded him and his preachers, or offered their houses for him to find rest and to read and write in – a wonderful tradition of Christian hospitality. We all 'tut! tut!' when the Apostolic Father writes of being saved by 'faith and hospitality', but if any people could be saved that way it might plausibly be the Methodists. And his Helpers – the clergy from the Perronets to Coke and Fletcher, and those lay assistants from John Nelson to Adam Clarke, not officer class but officer material; like Nelson's captains, a band of brothers, like Napoleon's marshals, able to make war on their own.

And then, the ladies. In 1959 Dr W. F. Lofthouse wrote two fine articles about them.[43]

It is certain [said Alexander Knox] that Mr Wesley had a predilection for the female character, . . . finding in females a quicker and fuller responsiveness to his own ideas of interior piety and affectionate devotion.[44]

It was the tradition of John Bradford and John Knox, of Francis of Sales and Fénelon. Partly no doubt, as Jean Guitton has said, because writing to ladies lessens the pain of writing letters. But it was a few of these – Mary Bishop, Hannah Ball, and Mary Bosanquet – who understood and used the *Christian Library*; as devout women had best understood St Bernard and Meister Eckhart and John Tauler in other centuries in that succession of a ministry of women which goes back to Galilee and for which Protestantism has taken too little heed and thought. And not only individuals but bands, classes, societies, devout companies.

Having in recent days re-read all the Journals and all the Letters from beginning to end, I cannot but say a word about the Old Wesley. Certainly we cannot drive a wedge between the Old Wesley and the Young, and the continuities are plain to see.

> I cannot write a better sermon on the Good Steward than I did seven years ago; [he wrote in 1778] I cannot write a better on the Great Assize than I did twenty years ago; I cannot write a better on the Use of Money than I did nearly thirty years ago; nay, I know not that I can write a better on the Circumcision of the Heart than I did five-and-forty years ago. . . . Forty years ago I knew and preached every Christian doctrine which I preach now.[45]

And if during those last years he could be querulous, sentimental, autocratic, there is overall a wonderfully appealing picture of a good, kind, holy, affectionate saint, breathing the love of God and of his fellow men. In those years, too, he had become an honoured national figure, whom William Wilberforce and John Howard sought out, and for whom old General Oglethorpe in his eighties stooped to kiss his hand.

We see him in his great age, bare-headed in the snow on four successive bitter winter mornings, begging from door to door in London, his feet always immersed in melting slush – but not stopping until he had begged two hundred pounds with which to feed and clothe his poor.

And, unforgettably, that last visit to Cornwall, to the town of Falmouth:

> The last time I was here, above forty years ago [at 86 he had forgotten he had been there twice since] I was taken prisoner by an immense mob, gaping and roaring like lions. But how is the tide turned! High and low now lined the street, from one end of the town to the other, out of stark love and kindness, gaping and staring as if the King were going by.[46]

No, not a King, but assuredly a very great ambassador.

9

Newman through Nonconformist Eyes*

I live by admiration, hope, and love, and Newman has always
inspired me with all these feelings toward himself and toward
many of his works. So much so, that I intend this little essay of
mine to be more of the nature of an acknowledgment and a
tribute than anything else. An acknowledgment, that is, of what
I owe of enlargement and enrichment of heart to this great
author.[1]

THAT JOHN HENRY NEWMAN cast a spell over minds
far beyond the bounds of the Church of England and the Church
of Rome has long been recognized. He was on any showing a
great man in a century of giants and, like Abraham Lincoln and
David Livingstone, had admirers of many creeds. Indeed, I do not
doubt it would be possible to compose a paper on 'Newman and
unbelievers' and to bring the tributes of many of no faith at all
in that age of half belief and unbelief who were in his debt. A
great man – a great man of letters ('guardian angel of the English
language', one admirer called him) – a saint. Do these things explain it? To press the inquiry to its deepest levels the witnesses
from Victorian nonconformity are relevant.

In the complex pattern of Victorian society, the nonconformists were important. Though not entirely freed from the
repressions and exclusions of a century and a half of persecution
and social ostracism, they were prosperous, independent, and
self-confident : important enough for government to take notice
of them, especially the Tapers and the Tadpoles at the time of a
general election : 'The Wesleyans – don't forget the Wesleyans'
cries somebody in Disraeli's *Sybil*. Sharing the good fortunes of a
prosperous section of the middle class of which they came near to

* A Paper delivered in April 1966 at the Oxford Newman Symposium;
and later published in J. Coulsdon and A. M. Allchin (eds), *The Rediscovery
of Newman* (London 1967)

being an establishment, with their new buildings, their crowded congregations, their great pulpiteers, they were by reason of these things still to some extent self-contained. Bigger than the older Dissenting Churches put together, in the first half of the century the Methodists held a middle position. They called themselves, and were not then offended when others called them 'the Body', and in the great matter of disestablishment it is important that as a whole the Methodists would not throw their weight against the Established Church. But it was the Catholic revival which very rapidly flung the Wesleyans and the older nonconformists into the Free Churches and formed the formidable nonconformist alliance of the last half of the nineteenth century.

This increases the puzzle of Newman. It is easy to account for nonconformist indifference, hostility, and prejudice, but the intriguing question is to account for the appreciation and admiring affection. They did not read him for his English alone – nor yet for his moralism – as they also read their Carlyle and their Ruskin. Somewhere below the ecclesiastical and cultural differences, deep called unto deep and heart spoke to heart. But let us begin with the fact, of which Father Ryder wrote :

> It is wonderful the extent to which of late years all sorts of persons with religious difficulties have had recourse to him. Members, often ministers, of various religious bodies, Methodists, Presbyterians, &c., with no sort of leaning towards the Church, have sought his guidance and advice and sympathy;... Indeed, now and again one came across something which almost looked like a *cultus* of Cardinal Newman outside the Church.[2]

And he goes on to tell how in a large manufacturing town a Baptist minister had preached for three Sundays on Cardinal Newman as a model of Christian virtue and used as his text an exposition of 'Lead, kindly light . . .'.

I propose to give you the testimonies of four eminent nonconformist divines for and against Newman, and then to look at those elements in Newman's life and thought which to a surprising degree speak to the heart of Evangelical Protestantism.

The Rev. Dr James Rigg (1821–1909) was a Worthy of nineteenth-century Wesleyan Methodism. He was twice President of the Conference and, as first principal of Westminster Training

College for Teachers (recently and happily translated to Oxford), he was much occupied in educational affairs. Not only did he know all the leading figures in the nonconformist world, but his pious biographer informs us that 'he enjoyed the confidence of four successive Archbishops of Canterbury'. As Mr Gladstone said in 1875, to coin a phrase, 'That Rigg is an able man . . . one of the ablest men I have met in committee'. In the light of what I am going to say it should be said that he was not of the straitest sect of the Evangelicals, and that in the matter of Church and education he refused to take the nonconformist line but remained true to the old high Wesleyan tradition. All the same, intellectually the mid-Victorian Methodists were an undistinguished lot – in contrast with the generation of Watson, Clarke, and Bunting.

Rigg was the author of several books. His most considerable work, written at the age of thirty-six, was *Modern Anglican Theology*, an all-out attack on the theology of Frederick Denison Maurice and his circle, whom he accused of poisoning the pure waters of Evangelical doctrine with a neo-Platonism deriving from Coleridge. Its chief value today is that it is a vast armoury of quotations not only from Maurice, but also from Kingsley, Julius Hare and Jowett.

In later life, Dr Rigg (and not least after the appearance of the *Apologia*) came to think more highly of Kingsley with whom he corresponded, and he struck up a friendship with his neighbour at Westminster, Dean Stanley. Now Kingsley was a great man, or at least Maurice-Kingsley made a great man like Chester-Belloc, and we lose the poignancy of the great debate if we play down Kingsley's great qualities and virtues or dismiss him simply as a second-rate thinker and writer, as the chief exponent of 'muscular Christianity'. But that cult did exist, and how very grisly it could be, we find when we turn to the writings about the Catholic revival of Dr Rigg.

It was in the 1880s that Rigg turned his literary attention to the Oxford Movement. By this time he had become the spokesman of a self-confident, self-conscious Wesleyanism, deriding openly the idea of reunion with the Church of England in terms of absorption. But the sharpest edge of his mind, which perhaps was no Wilkinson sword blade at that, was towards the reviving of Popery. He led the group which induced the Methodist

Church to draw up a new service of baptism in the 1880s, the express purpose of which was to exclude baptismal regeneration. Though one of the moderate Evangelicals he found himself in deep agreement with the Protestant underworld's best seller, Walsh's *Secret History of the Oxford Movement*, and, though his own *Oxford High Anglicanism* was more restrained and less sensational, he sold enough copies to be able to publish an enlarged edition four years later in which he deplored that 'Romanising neo-Anglicanism which would...have sorely changed for the worse the morality and manly virtue of our nation'.

His writings against Maurice and Newman and their friends are a sad, because entirely unconscious, revelation of the extent to which the English Evangelical tradition stood itself in need of refreshment. I need not enter into the rigidities of its doctrine, but turn at once to what he has to say about Newman. The curious key of his criticism is found in a note to page 13 on 'The Feminine Vein in Newman's Character':

> Newman was not, indeed, effeminate; but he seems to have been without any specially masculine tastes, pursuits, or passions.... He was addicted to no specially manly exercises. He was not an athlete, he had no tastes in that direction...[3]

and this is a common quality, he thinks, of the pioneers of the Oxford Movement:

> ...[the friendships] of Newman and his circle were passionately deep and warm...more like those of women who live aloof from the world in the seclusion of mutual intimacy....[4]

> Newman's was a characteristically feminine nature; it was feminine in the quickness and subtlety of his instincts, in affection and the caprices of affection,...in a gift of statement and grace of phrase which find their analogies in the conversation, in the public addresses, and even in the written style of gifted women. He was wanting in virility, in manly strength, and we cannot easily accept as a great man anyone who is not a truly manly man....[5]

> With Newman, as with people of a commoner sort, feelings, prepossessions, prejudices, determined the creed; his logic was

ever an afterthought and a mere instrument of defence or persuasion . . . a characteristically feminine mind, poetic, impressible, receptive, and reproductive, rather than original and commanding; and with the feminine mind was joined a feminine temperament.[6]

One feels that Dr Rigg might at least have considered the possibility of considering Newman, if not as the Grand Old Man, at least as the Grand Old Woman of the nineteenth century, and to have placed him with Jane Austen, Harriet Martineau, and Miss Nightingale and the Brontës, as fit to rank at least in some immortal Parthenon.

Another point for Rigg was Newman's worldliness. Were not cricket and other games played in the Oratory School at Birmingham on Sunday with noises offensive to pious nonconformist ears? And then there were violins, and other music.

He was diligent in reading his *Times* daily, following with keen curiosity public affairs . . . in editing Latin plays for the Oratory boys to act, and in taking the part of theatrical manager . . . of costumes and scenery.[7]

Influential as Rigg was, and representative as he was of one section, and not the narrowest of Victorian Evangelical opinion, the next generation of Methodists, of Hugh Price Hughes and John Scott Lidgett were of a more catholic temper. Lidgett succeeded Rigg in the field of educational statesmanship, and though a leader in the Free Church partnership, was an architect of Methodist Union, and a founding father of the Ecumenical Movement. As a young divine, he refused even to read Rigg's attack on his hero, Frederick Denison Maurice, and I suspect he had as little patience with Rigg's *Oxford High Anglicanism*. He himself embodied what we must now call the 'holy worldliness' which Rigg had so deplored in Newman : for he became Vice-Chancellor of London University, Chairman of the LCC, and founder of the Bermondsey settlement, very proud to be the first Methodist minister to be licensed to sell tobacco and run a billiard saloon. At the heart of Lidgett's religion was the Nicene Faith. And in his memoirs he tells how deep upon him was the influence of Newman's writings, especially his writings about the Early Church.[8]

Alexander Whyte spoke for others who shared this debt when he wrote:

> No one can feel the full force of Newman's great sermons on 'The Incarnation', and on 'The Atoning Death of God the Son', who has not gone with Newman ... up to the sources of the sermons in Athanasius, and in Basil, and in Cyril. The greatest and the most sure to be lasting of Newman's sermons are just his rich Athanasian Christology poured into the mould of his incomparable homiletic, ... [9]

And in contrast with Pearson on the Creed, Whyte adds:

> Newman delivers all his readers ever after from a cold, dry, notional, technical, catechetical mind, he so makes every article of the Creed a very fountain of life and power and beauty. He so lifts up his own superb imagination to its noblest use, that he makes, first himself, and then makes us to see, the Divine Persons, and their Divine relations and operations, as never before. Till all our Creeds and Confessions and Catechisms become clothed with a majesty, and instinct with a beauty, and welling over with personal applications and comforts, new, and unexpected, and ever-abiding. [10]

But however much the Victorians rejoiced in the light, whether of reason or of faith, they were all to some degree conscious of the encircling gloom. We need always to remember the polarities of optimism and pessimism, of belief and unbelief and half belief, the corrosion of older certainties in minds like Carlyle and Froude and Ruskin, the muted trumpets of 'In Memoriam'. From some of this the nonconformist world was isolated and insulated, still to an extent a 'garden walled around', still confident in an earlier rational apologetic, of Butler and Paley. I would not exaggerate this, but I think it is true that Victorian Evangelicalism knew little of that razor edge between faith and unbelief, the long tradition of *Anfechtung* from Luther to Kierkegaard. It was natural for such to find in Newman an incomprehensible surrender of the intellect. One who is controversy and argument showed a mind so keen, sensitive beyond most, aware of the subtlest inferences – from this to the Holy Coat of Treves and the sacred House at Loreto, and to many of them, the hardly more reputable notions of Infallibility and the Mario-logical dogmas, this seemed indeed a surrender.

Moreover, Newman had a drastic way with half-way houses, not only in regard to the paper defences of a *Via Media*, but, as he explicitly stated in his essay on John Keble, that the alternatives might in the end be Rome, or rationalism. If for Luther reason was the devil's whore, Frau Hulda, Newman was almost as trenchant in his description of reason as the instrument of the world, of what St Paul called the wisdom of this world.

These things explain the superficial plausibility of the charge of scepticism brought against Newman in 1885 by the Congregationalist divine, Andrew Fairbairn.[11] He was a scholar of growing distinction, at this time the Principal Designate of the new Mansfield College, Oxford, one who helped greatly in forming theological faculties in the Universities of Manchester and Wales. As a scholar, he was not to be despised. He was a considerable theologian, a Free Churchman with the blood of the Scottish Covenanters in his veins. But he was also a fine teacher, to whom many students owed their souls, and a preacher of whom some Methodist fishermen once said, 'He did talk to we like an angel'.

For him the traditional proofs of the existence of God, and notably the argument from design were of great importance, and it was particularly this proof about which Newman had reservations which he never abandoned. So that Fairbairn's mind was puzzled and affronted by the *Grammar of Assent*. In an article in the *Contemporary Review*, May 1885, he asserted that the *Grammar* 'was pervaded by the intensest philosophical scepticism'. Newman's philosophy he asserted may be described as 'empirical and sceptical, qualified by a peculiar religious experience'. 'He has a deep distrust of the intellect . . . he dares not trust his own, for he does not know where it might lead him, and he will not trust any other man's.' To what he called Fairbairn's 'vehement rhetoric', Newman replied in an article in the same review in October, with politeness, if you discount the evident fact that Newman had not the slightest interest in Fairbairn or his opinions, but was only concerned with what his own friends might think. In December, Fairbairn returned to the charge that 'to conceive reason as Dr Newman does is to deny to it the knowledge of God, and so to save faith by the help of a deeper unbelief'.[12]

Newman consulted his friends about writing anything further in public admitting that 'it would require a very brilliant knock down answer to Dr F. to justify my giving up my place "as an *emeritus miles* and going down into the arena with a younger man'. What he did was to publish privately some footnotes, which appeared as the third part of *Stray Essays on Controversial Points*, short, pointed, luminous paragraphs.[13]

He had no difficulty in disposing of the charge, which in fact Dr Fairbairn had no notion of preferring, that he was a 'hidden sceptic' – 'for a long seventy years amid mental trials sharp and heavy, I can in my place and in my measure adopt the words of St Polycarp before his martyrdom'. He also made plain the sense in which he spoke of the faculty of reason, and the reason for his denunciation of it when it became what St Paul calls 'the wisdom of this world'.

It is plain that there was genuine misunderstanding. It is also, I think, plain that Newman's answer is not completely convincing. But Fairbairn's biographer, Dr Selbie, is surely right when he says that 'the two men were working on different planes and using language each in a way that was hardly intelligible to the other'.

Perhaps the best footnote is to remember that in the course of this controversy, Fairbairn paid the following tribute to his adversary :

> It costs a very peculiar kind of suffering to conduct a controversy, after his personal intervention, with the one man in all England on whose lips the words of the dying Polycarp sit with equal truth and grace. Not that Cardinal Newman has been either a hesitating or a soft-speaking controversialist. He has been a man of war from his youth, who has conquered many adversaries. . . . He has, as scarcely any other teacher of our age, made us feel the meaning of life, the evil of sin, the dignity of obedience, the beauty of holiness : and his power has been due to the degree in which men have been constrained to believe that his words, where sublimest, have been but the dim and imperfect mirrors of his own exalted spirit. . . . He has greatly and variously enriched the religious life of our people, and he lives in our imagination as the last at once of the Fathers and of the Saints.[14]

So far, I have spoken of nonconformists who were admirers

of Newman. In Alexander Whyte, Newman had, in Kierkegaard's phrase, a lover. Alexander Whyte (1836–1921) was
one of the really great figures of the Scottish Church in the nineteenth century, and his life by G. F. Barbour, an outstanding
biography,[15] the reading of which must have been for many a
theological student, as for me, a climacteric event. Whyte was
born in J. M. Barrie's 'Thrums', the little Forfarshire town of
Kirriemuir, a kind of Victorian Tannochbrae, but one where
doctors of divinity counted for more than men of medicine and
where the tensions between Drs Cameron, Finlay, and the egre-
gious Dr Snoddy were as nothing compared with the suspicious
rivalries of Auld Licht, Wee Frees, and Episcopalians. From this
unpromising and unecumenical setting, Alexander Whyte went
forth to become in due season Principal of New College of Edinburgh; but his real fame was as a preacher, as the famous minister of St George's, Edinburgh.

It was as a preacher that he was drawn to Newman, and as a
preacher he understood him, so that his little book on Newman
has insights into Newman missed by Father Bouyer. Whyte's
generation did not despise its inherited Reformed Calvinism, but
there was an opening up to new influences, Hegel in philosophy,
and in theology the Greek Fathers. And then Whyte came from
that part of north-east Scotland where in the seventh as in the
seventeenth century theology and mysticism have ever blended.
The lectures, which over many years he delivered to his people
of Edinburgh, covered a wide range of Protestant and Catholic
spirituality, Dante and Tauler being especially beloved. From unpromising beginnings Whyte grew to a true Catholicity, and thus
he defined the true Catholic :

> How rich such men are . . . for all things are theirs. All men, and
> all books, and all churches. Whether Paul, or John, or Augustine,
> or Athanasius, or Dante, or Behmen, or Luther, or Calvin, or
> Hooker, or Taylor, or Knox, or Rutherford, or Bunyan, or Butler,
> or Edwards, or Chalmers, or Newman, or Spurgeon. And we have
> not a few of such Catholic Evangelicals in our pulpits, and among
> our people in Scotland, and they are mutliplying among us every
> day.[16]

There were three points of personal contact between Whyte and

Newman. The first was the visit which, with two friends, Dr
Marcus Dods and Dr Thomason, he paid to the Oratory.

> In those days of entrenched Protestantism it needed no small
> courage for three Free Churchmen, who were still young in the
> ministry to go on pilgrimage to the Oratory.

Shyly they entered, though they did not fail to notice the large
violincello propped against the wall.

> He received us with all that captivating urbanity which has be-
> come proverbial :... the old saint treating us in all that with a
> frankness and with a confidence as if we were old friends of his, as
> indeed we were.[17]

When Whyte was married in 1881, his wife gave him a portrait
of Newman and wrote asking Newman for his autograph. Newman replied thanking her

> for what you say about the interest which Dr Whyte takes in
> my writings, which suggests the hope and trust that, in spite of
> the sad divisions of Christendom, a great work is going on in the
> hearts of serious men, tending towards a restoration of the scat-
> tered members of Christ, even though not in our day, yet in the
> future, in 'the times and seasons which He has appointed'.[18]

Newman enclosed four autographs and a few days later wrote to
ask whether what he had sent would do. Barbour asked, 'Could
the fine gold of Christian courtesy be further refined than this?'
Henceforth his portrait hung in a place of honour in Whyte's
study, between pictures of Carlyle and Herschel (as one has hung
in my own study for thirty years – between Luther and Karl
Barth !).

In 1883 Whyte published a short commentary on the Catechism, and sent a copy to Newman. Newman replied courteously,
but took exception to Whyte's assertion that the doctrine of
transubstantiation meant that 'all communicants literally and
physically eat the flesh and drink the blood of Christ'. Newman
asserted that 'not the most ignorant or stupid Catholic thinks
that he eats physically the body of our Lord'. Whyte at once
accepted Newman's explanation and asked him to draft a line

which appeared to state the correct Catholic view, and when Newman expanded his objection in a further letter, he offered to print the letter itself in a further edition. To this last suggestion Newman demurred on the ground that 'it would be a poor return on my part to your courteous treatment of me in your book, to turn your catechism into a controversy'.

Whyte's sentence, amended to the judgment of Newman, appeared in the new form in the second edition. But the last word was a letter from Newman, whose conscience had been troubled as he had himself been disarmed, by Whyte's charitable handling, to say that it was very likely that the framers of the Catechism had in mind 'extreme notions of the *multitude* who were in many places superstitious and sadly in want of instruction'.[19] Here in 1884 is the very spirit of *De Ecumenismo* and a reminder that we who like to think of ourselves as the pioneers of ecumenicity are in fact the epigoni of men like Lidgett and Alexander Whyte.

Whyte had read every printed syllable of Newman's writings. He had, for example, read and reread all the *Tracts for the Times.* He spoke with approval of an old Scottish carpenter who was wont, as a devotional exercise, simply to read through the titles of the *Parochial and Plain Sermons,* and he himself wrote to a young student :

Take a volume of first-rate sermons – Newman, or Robertson, or Parker, or Spurgeon, etc. – and enter the texts of a whole volume.[20]

To another he wrote :

I am better pleased with your teaching than with your style. You should rewrite this discourse, and ask as you write – would Newman have used this and that expression in a sermon?[21]

In his seventieth year he wrote to one of his children :

I wrote my last forenoon sermon three times over. And that is the only thing in which I resemble Newman. He wrote *all* his sermons as often as I wrote mine last week.[22]

But it was not just as a craftsman that he was drawn to Newman as a master. It was, says Barbour,

Newman's constant and all-pervading conviction of the presence
of God in the life of man, his awed sense of the insignificance of
all earthly interests in comparison with the moral and religious
issues which reach out into eternity, his delicate but searching
analysis of the hidden processes of good and evil in the heart, his
reverence of spirit, and the quiet perfection of his English style,[23]

which effected an effortless mastery over an ear and conscience
so sensitively attuned as those of Alexander Whyte.

Whyte's criticisms of Newman are trenchant, and were only
published after Newman's death, but they are to be taken seriously against the background of his admiration and his love. His
criticism of the sermons is that they are under the Law.

> Looked at as pure literature, Newman's St Mary's sermons are
> not far from absolute perfection; but looked at as pulpit work,
> as preaching the Gospel, they are full of the most serious, and
> even fatal, defects. With all their genius . . . they are not, properly
> speaking, New Testament preaching at all. . . . As an analysis of
> the heart of man, and as a penetrating criticism of human life,
> their equal is nowhere to be found. But . . . they lack the one all-
> essential element of true preaching – the message to sinful man
> concerning the free grace of God. That message was the one
> thing that differentiated the Apostle's preaching from all the
> other so-called preaching of his day. And that one thing which
> has been the touchstone of all true preaching ever since the
> Apostle's day, and will be to the end of the world, that is all but
> totally lacking in Newman's sermons.[24]

> Moses was never dressed up in such ornaments before. . . . The
> old lawgiver would not know himself, he is so beautified and be-
> decked by Newman's style. But, all the time, he is Moses. All the
> time, with all his ornaments, he still carries his whip of scorpions
> hidden away among his beautiful garments. Do and live! Dis-
> obey and die! and he draws his sword on me as he says it. . . .
> I have given not a few of Newman's books to young men in
> other circumstances, and at other stages . . . but never one of his
> beautiful books to a broken-hearted and inconsolable sinner. I
> have often given to men in dead earnest, books of the heart and
> soul that Newman and his Tractarian school would scorn to
> name.[25]

And Whyte gives a list of Puritan and Evangelical classics of devotion from Bunyan down to Spurgeon and Ryle. And he goes on to say that, while he has often and gladly recommended Newman's writings, he could never recommend either his *Lectures on Justification* or the *Sermons* to a penitent whose sins had found him out.

Newman was the Rembrandt of a Tractarian school at the heart of which was theological chiaroscuro. The darkness was Protestantism, the errors of the Reformers, and to compare Newman with John Adam Möhler is to feel that Anglo-Catholic polemic had, in this regard, obtusenesses and blind spots and rigidities beyond those of the Church of Rome. Whyte, with his love of Puritan and Protestant divinity, could not but be constantly wounded by Newman's deadly ironies and his occasional devastating contempt. Recalling how, in 1843, Newman had issued a formal retractation of all the hard things which he had said against the Church of Rome, he wished that in 1890 Newman had retracted all his

> slings and scoffs ... at men whose shoe-latchet, he should have said, he was not worthy to unloose ... such men of God as Luther, and Calvin, and the Anglican Reformers, as well as Bunyan, and Newton, and Wesley, ... men to whom their Master will yet say, Well done, good and faithful servant! and that, too, in Newman's hearing.[26]

Well, it is blessedly true that

> And sometimes even beneath the moon,
> The Saviour gives a gracious boon,
> When reconcilèd Christians meet.[27]

But Whyte perhaps asked too much of the nineteenth-century sublunary pieties. We remember how in Dante's *Paradiso* those who were unreconciled, theological enemies on earth go out of their way to do honour to their former adversaries. And if, in the light of glory, St Thomas can lead forward Siger of Brabant, then we may expect Newman in the forefront of such heavenly ecumenicities.

That, in my study, Newman's portrait should rest between those of Luther and Karl Barth may seem offensive to pious eyes, I know. My own copy of the *Lectures on Justification* I have underscored and annotated on every page and almost every paragraph, and question and exclamation marks abound. But the testimonies I have brought forward point to a common Christian core, that fundamental unity in Christ which is the starting point rather than the goal of the search for visible unity.

Then there is the well known fact of the deep continuities in the religion of Newman himself, from his Evangelical upbringing through his Anglican ministry to the Church of Rome. To the end of his life he continued to republish those Oxford sermons; so little did he need to repudiate, so that the recent Catholic anthology *The Heart of Newman*[28] draws its most splendid passages from this pre-Roman source. Let us forget for a moment the polemic and ponder one or two remarkable similarities.

Here is a University movement; its core a group of younger scholars and teachers. It is involved in a crisis in which a whole contemporary culture is concerned, so that it is at once a protest against the present, and a bid for the allegiance of a coming age. At its nerve centre is one man, head and shoulders above his fellows, a man, like Shaw's St Joan, in love with religion, over whose life might be inscribed the text, 'The zeal of thine house has eaten me up'. It is he who pens one after another their manifestoes, and upon whose head the disapproval of authority descends. And this, unlooked for; for he is the most unwilling, the most obedient of rebels, and in his protest had hoped for and looked for the support of his ecclesiastical superiors. But one by one they fail, until at last, disowned and discredited by those leaders from whom he hoped so much – he takes the final, fatal step of rebellion : he steps outside his Church.

Every word of that paragraph applied equally to Martin Luther and to John Henry Newman, and I would there were time to bring dozens of citations from the writings of both men during the critical, fateful months of their development, to show the rapidity of their mental growth, their anguished hypersensitivity and sometimes perhaps a theological arrogance, the more terrible because so impersonal, so free from pride and personal vanity, to demonstrate all the intricate similarities between the utterances of the one between 1517 and 1521 and the other between 1841 and 1845. Both men stand for the opposite of what is now called 'religionless Christianity' as reminders that, despite all the gravity of divine judgment, God never disavows his

People, that for their renewal he ever sends his champions, and that they are almost without exception those to whom he has given the terrible and beautiful calling of being religious men, ecclesiastics, and theologians.

Luther and Newman were preachers, of each of whom it could be said that the pulpit was their throne, the secret of their ascendancy over the minds of men, and their writings but powerful extensions of their sermons. Of both it might be said, as Karl Holl said about Luther, that theirs was above all a religion of conscience. Who between Luther and Newman, and apart from them, could ground the Priesthood of Believers here and not in ecclesiology?

> Conscience is the aboriginal Vicar of Christ, a prophet in its informations, a monarch in its peremptoriness, a priest in its blessings and anathemas, and even though the eternal priesthood throughout the Church could cease to be, in it the sacerdotal principle would remain and would have a sway.[29]

Both mastered words to the point of genius and did so because both were poets, and indeed musicians. Both were great polemic divines, writing as occasion moved them, so that Whyte speaks for Luther as well as Newman when he comments on the way in which

> his passions largely decide and fix his standing-ground for the time; and, then, how his imagination ... and his argumentative talents ... all come in to fortify, and to defend, and to make warlike and aggressive, every present position of his.[30]

Poor Kingsley! Poor Erasmus!

And then, Luther was a much gentler person than most people dream, or than you would gather from his polemic, and I think there may be this speck of truth in what Rigg's essay says about Newman having a feminine mind though, if so, it is also true of Luther, that both think with their imaginations, and teem with beautiful and profound intuitions, and it is these, rather than their logic, which hold us – seven times out of ten wonderfully right – and then in the next breath utterly and disastrously wrong with the other three (a quality of our late and beloved Gregory Dix).

Nineteenth-century Evangelicalism was further from Calvin than it knew, and its Calvin something infected by its passage from the age of William Perkins through the eighteenth-century Evangelical tradition – as any comparison between Karl Barth and modern Evangelicalism reveals. But it is Calvin's lucid clarities in French and Latin which come nearer to Newman than Luther, and both share, perhaps even one inherited from another, two fundamentals of their theology. You remember Newman's famous statement of how in his youth his mind came to rest in

the thought of two and two only absolute and luminously self-evident beings, myself and my Creator – [31]

so close to the magnificent opening of Calvin's masterpiece:

The whole sum in a manner of all our wisdom, which only ought to be accounted true and perfect wisdom, consisteth in two parts, that is to say, the knowledge of God, and of ourselves.[32]

And the hall mark of both great divines is their reverence for God:

But if we once begin to raise up our thought unto God and to weigh what a one he is, and how exact is the perfection of his righteousness, wisdom and power, after the rule whereof we ought to be framed....[33]

How like the passage in the *Grammar of Assent* where Newman also bids us

contemplate the God of our conscience as a Living Being, as one Object and Reality ... we must patiently rest in the thought of the Eternal, Omnipresent, and All-knowing, ...[34]

And perhaps Newman's youthful conversion was nearer to Calvin than that of the Evangelicals, like John Wesley.

I may not stay to draw parallels, which you might think even more forced and outrageous between Newman and Zwingli – for there is a most interesting point at which Zwingli's hymn, 'The Plague' written during an almost fatal illness recalls Newman's 'Lead, Kindly Light' – both coming through to a trust in Providence: Zwingli's 'Lord I am thy vessel – make me or break me – ' and 'So long thy power hath blessed me . . .' And then John Wesley – though it might seem that all they had in common was that both were divines and Oxford dons – there might be some virtue in that 'all', beside the interesting junction which puts Alexander Knox halfway between them both, for both were theologically linked with the Father of Irish Ecumenicity.

I myself would distinguish rather sharply between the doctrines of the Reformers and what nineteenth-century Protestants conceived to be the Principles of the Reformation. But when modern German and French Catholic scholars stress the individualism of Newman, they have in mind surely such passages as this in which Newman puts what many Protestants conceive to be the real meaning of the Priesthood of all Believers, the fact that none may stand between the soul and God :

> This I know full well, . . . that the Catholic Church allows no image of any sort, material or immaterial, no dogmatic symbol, no rite, no sacrament, no Saint, not even the Blessed Virgin herself, to come between the soul and its Creator. It is face to face, 'solus cum solo', in all matters between man and his God.[35]

In a well-known essay, G. K. Chesterton contrasted Bunyan's *Pilgrim's Progress* with *Canterbury Tales,* and criticized the loneliness of Pilgrim's way with the happy band of Canterbury Pilgrims. But the real comparison is between *Pilgrim's Progress* and the 'Dream of Gerontius', and the shuddering loneliness of Newman, which I am bound to say recalls for me the criticism of Alexander Whyte of Newman's sermons, at least at the point of death, when the encircling gloom is almost overpowering, and where the 'Dies Irae' prevails over *tantus labor non sit cassus.* I am not forgetting 'Praise to the Holiest' either, but I wonder whether it isn't Elgar in the end who saves the Christian balance. And then Newman's defence of Private Judgement – not in his polemical essay on the subject, but in places in the *Apologia* where he asserts there is an awful never-dying duel in the Church between Authority and Private Judgement – 'alternately advancing and retreating as the ebb and flow of the tide' : which if it irresistibly recalls the Mock Turtle and the Gryphon in *Alice* – 'will you, won't you, will you, won't you' – defends perhaps all that Protestants ought ever to have defended, apart from the grave questions of religious liberty and the duty to obey one's conscience.

I hope these are not forced parallels, a magnification of accidental resemblances. They seem to me some of the evidence for an ecumenical norm, a core of unity, stemming from our unity in baptism, from which in our time a dialogue might well begin. For there are these deep continuities in Newman himself, and they are not simply that, in spite of all temptations to belong to other nations, and perhaps Eye-talian – above all Eye-talian, he remained an Englishman. On the Continent let Hans Küng talk it out with Karl Barth, but in England let us begin with Newman. Begin with the *Lectures on the Prophetical Office of the Church*, and go on to the *Development* and the *Reply* to Pusey.

There is a story; it may be apocryphal, but it was told me by the grandson of one of the two concerned. Some time in the 1880s, two men sat side by side on a park bench in Birmingham. One was an old Methodist minister, a supernumerary, the other Cardinal Newman. They talked about the Church, and Newman took an umbrella and drew a circle in the dust. 'I think', he said, 'it is important to get the circumference right.' 'Ah', said the Methodist, taking the umbrella and poking a hole in the centre of the circle, 'we think that all that matters is the centre. Get that right and the circumference will come right too.' Well, in these days we must begin with the centre, with the Living Word of God from whom the Church is born. But the circumference matters too. *Securus judicat orbis terrarum*. And it is He, the Saviour of Mankind, who sits on the circumference of the earth, with all mankind compassed within the orbit of redeeming love.

Like the other Protestant observers at the Vatican, I as less than the least gratefully marvelled at the place of honour where we sat, but most appropriately of all, as it seemed to me, that we sat where day after day we could not but stare and ponder at one text of the many inscribed in gold high up in the nave – for I think it may be the key text for our ecumenical dialogue, heart-searching but inspiring in promise, glossing our thoughts of *aggiornamento* with the thought of *Ecclesia semper reformanda* – 'When thou art converted, strengthen thy brethren'.

10

Hort and the Cambridge Tradition*

MR VICE-CHANCELLOR,[1]
I ask pardon for not beginning this lecture with the customary tribute to my immediate predecessor. But perhaps I am absolved because the University has already paid tribute, *ex officio*, so to speak, to your distinction among us as a scholar and divine. For my further indiscretion in speaking in your presence of an episode in the life of the Victorian Church, I can only say with Thomas Fuller that 'next to the study of the Scriptures, history best becometh the gentleman, Church History a Christian, and the British history an Englishman, all which qualifications eminently meeting in your honour, give me some comfortable assurance that my weak endeavours will not be unwelcome to you'.

Sometimes, too, a new Professor will use such an occasion as this to look before and after at the provision made for his subject in the University, and its future needs. But I have rather recently returned to Cambridge with something of the dazed rapture of a Jacob who, having settled down happily, and as he thought permanently, with Leah, finds himself suddenly transferred to Rachel's bosom, as yet too stunned to have got round to counting sheep in Laban's household. Then, too, my predecessors were called into the vineyard at the sixth and at the ninth hour, with time enough to criticize the management, but I at the eleventh had better simply study to be a labourer worthy of his hire.

I think myself in duty bound to mention two of our predecessors : James Pounder Whitney, and Norman Sykes. I came to Professor Whitney in his rooms in this college, along with a nun and an inarticulate student from Iceland, in Whitney's last years, when the subjects discussed bore little relation to the Lecture List, though there were some splendid stories of his early

* An Inaugural Lecture delivered in the University of Cambridge on 14 November 1969 and published by Cambridge University Press.

6—JM * *

curacies which illuminated little-known aspects of ecclesiastical history in the nineteenth century.

But there was the stimulus of a great and kindly teacher, the evidence on the shelves around of the magnificent range of his learning. And as he talked about the Early Church, or the age of Hildebrand, or Wycliffe, or Erasmus, or Luther, one recognized something beyond versatility, that wholeness of Christian history, which it is the chief virtue of the exercise known as Section III of Part III of the Theological Tripos to deploy and which I have always considered the best possible course for a future teacher or writer of ecclesiastical history.

About Norman Sykes I find it more difficult to speak. I remember, long ago, going into a lecture room in King's College, London, and wondering whether the youngest lecturer in the History School would be as good as the little Benn's Sixpenny Library study, *Church and State in England since the Reformation*, which had just appeared and which like all his shorter books was a marvel of perceptive compression.

He seemed to his students a delightful compound of Leeds and Oxford, Parnassus and Heckmondwike, but they soon came to see beneath the Yorkshireman with his rough banter a sensitive spirit and a noble mind. His writings make a compact little fleet. Three or four short books, the frigates; four series of lectures, redoubtable 74s : then two 'ships of the line' – the Life of Bishop Gibson, and the double series of Birkbecks; *Church and State in England in the XVIIIth Century*, a *Fighting Téméraire* whose broadsides blew away an era of misconceptions. And the massive Life of Archbishop Wake – a huge *San Trinidad* which sometimes made heavy weather, but is likeliest of all to ride out the storm of time. The eighteenth century was his spiritual home, and such much of his energy went into writing about it that in comparison his Gunning, Wiles and Ford lectures are not their match. He rated the words of Samuel Johnson but little lower than Holy Scripture, literally, for some of his sermons seemed to have two texts, and what was latent in Holy Writ became patent in the pages of Boswell; but he liked also to quote George Herbert with whom he shared a deep and abiding love for the Church of England as a *via media*.

He had a wonderful eye for quotations generally, not least from Shakespeare and from W. S. Gilbert, and rather revealingly from the Latin Psalms. It is not fair to say that he was obtuse towards traditions other than his own, though the first note I had from him, after an examination, had the ironic comment : 'Of course I accept your refutation of my views on John Wesley.' But if he had more sympathy with Bishop Butler and even with Beau Nash than with the Wesleyan historians, at least he had none of the sour incomprehension of recent sociological Jabberwocks who delight to bite and claw at the evangelical story. And, like all the holders of the Dixie Chair, he knew that this English language of ours is first and foremost a musical instrument – and never a blunt tool, not a cosh, not a bulldozer. And if it be true that the 'Church of England what it is, none but its lovers know', then perhaps the first non-Anglican holder of this Chair might claim to be among those lovers, and not least because those who taught him church history were Church of England men, such as Norman Sykes and Charles Smyth, who brought him face to face with its incomparable tradition of sound learning. It is within that tradition I would speak to you of Fenton John Anthony Hort.

It was of great moment for Hort and for Cambridge scholarship when in 1872 the Fellows of Emmanuel took advantage of a recent statute enabling them to elect a person eminent in letters or science, 'etiamsi uxorem duxerit'. As lecturer in divinity in this college in the twenty years that followed, Hort amply repaid the generous gesture, and took the closest interest in the arrangements which led in 1882 to the founding of the Dixie Chair, so that it was founded, as Whitney said, along lines laid down by Hort, and expressed Hort's ideas of what History and Theology could be and do when linked together.[2]

What needs to be said of Hort as a New Testament scholar, and of his association with Lightfoot and Westcott at Trinity, and what all of them owed to that college, has been lucidly summarized in recent months by Bishop Stephen Neill.[3] Those who want to know about Hort will find the *Life and Letters* by his son one of the more engaging of Victorian lives,[4] while if you want the full quality of his mind you may read, as some still re-read, as a not so minor spiritual classic, his Hulsean Lectures, *The Way, the Truth, the Life*.

Some facts about the man must be borne in mind if we would understand his attitude towards Ecclesiastical History. In the days following his death in November 1892 his friends recalled the vivid image of his presence :

> The familiar sight of the man, with the quick, nervous step, the left arm folded across books and papers, the right swinging vigorously across the body as he hurried down Trumpington Street – or as he rounded at full pace some buttress of books in the University Library.

At closer quarters

> the wonderful blue eyes, piercing keenly beneath the penthouse of a bushy brow, the worn emaciated cheek, the noble forehead, the bright glee of his merriment, the tremendous energy.[5]

He seems to have been one of those who must be always on the stretch, who are the joy and worry of their friends because they live at the edges of their nerves and energy. And it was the enormous range of Hort's zestful interests, and the many-sidedness of his great endowments of mind and spirit, which brought with them the defects of their virtues.

But how various were those gifts and interests! Robbed of the inevitable First in Mathematics by a virus fever which left permanent mark, he went on to take three Firsts in Classics, Moral Philosophy and Natural Sciences (with distinctions in Physiology and Botany) – finding time to be President of the Union, and incidentally in debate to denounce that 'bad historian' and 'wretched imposter', Lord Macaulay. He had also more than his share of academic disappointments. In the golden age of the do-gooder he was lavish in attention to causes. Devoted to Maurice – he coined the word 'Maurikizein' – and to Kingsley, he was never swept into the Christian Socialist camp. But in this city, where a Chartist demonstration failed to compete with the cricket balls on Parker's Piece, he helped found the first Working Men's College in a room behind the Market Place. In the middle of a serious breakdown, and when Lightfoot and Westcott were gloomily begrudging the time Hort was devoting to lumping bits of rock all over the Cotswolds, he could say in an aside : 'I am attending to nine treasurers' accounts besides my own.' In the 1880s, apart from the immense labour of editing the Revised Version, of which he was the king, he attended innumerable committees, in Cambridge alone 207 sessions – averaging two and three-quarter hours each.

And yet at this time he could correspond with his Wesleyan friend, Dr Moulton of the Leys, about mending a roof, or finding a new kitchen maid for the Perse School for Girls. And besides all these things, he was a great doer in the University, examiner for three or four Triposes, concerned for University extension, involved in reading manuscripts for the Press Syndicate and in affairs of the Library. Music he loved, and he wrote hymns – hated barrel organs and prophesied that the Church would one day use the dance in worship. Poetry he wrote and literature he devoured in that decent age when people still read aloud to one another. He had a lively concern for issues of the day and if he attacked the new Theological Tripos it was for the best of reasons : that theology only really flourishes when it is pursued alongside other disciplines, and that it must never become an isolated, specialist, or merely technical study.

Perhaps because like Maurice he put Church above party and perhaps because Cambridge was not Oxford, his judgments about contemporary ecclesiastical history are always worth considering – while he has a page on the character of Newman as shrewd as anything ever written about him.[6] Only in foreign affairs did he miss out; and there are some terrible lines about the Negroes which may betray the disastrous influence of Kingsley's racism : 'I hate slavery . . . much more for its influence on the whites than on the niggers themselves . . . they have surely shown themselves only as an immeasurably inferior race, just human and no more, their religion frothy and sensuous, their highest virtues those of a good Newfoundland dog.' About which one can only say, as Ruskin said of Harriet Martineau, he was 'not a villain but a goose'.

Despite Arnold's interest in the subject, Hort had little interest in history at Rugby and came to it late in his Cambridge studies, so that in some ways he is one of the last of the great amateurs. But he came to believe it was of the utmost importance :

> The history of the Church from its foundation to the present hour is hardly less necessary to the Church at large than the gospel itself . . . doubtless for the Church as for the first disciples what lies before differs widely from what lies behind : but that

which runs through both alike is the one way ... to be traced alike in the successes and failures of the past and to be followed unflinchingly through whatsoever unlooked-for windings as it leads among the unfolding hopes or fears of the ages yet to come.

For Hort this involved not only the continuity and wholeness of church history, but the consideration of the background, what he called the entire historical 'landscape'. He criticized a project for spanning church history in a series of biographies:

> There is a great inclination in the present day to resolve history into biography plus geography – which seems to me almost purely mischievous – it destroys all essential continuity – you will never be able to make history by stringing biographies in a row, let them fit on to each other never so closely.

Most striking of all is his letter, at the end of 1852, when he was twenty-four:

> My thoughts have for some time converged towards making Church History the central object of my reading, with a view perhaps to writing a great history years hence, especially containing a full landscape, foreground and background of the times, independently of religious and ecclesiastical matters. But the necessary preparation will be enormous. Independently of the entire contemporary literature, sacred and profane, and all the principal comments and digests of the same from the fifteenth century until now, I shall have to devote great labour to discovering and constructing an accurate view of the world in all its aspects (especially the social) before the coming of Christ.[7]

And he goes on to explain that this grand design would also include writing the entire history of the Jews from Abraham to 300 B.C., the history of Greek philosophy and its relation to Hellenic culture; and the history of the Hellenic world from the death of Alexander the Great to the birth of Christ.

Well, no doubt as a programme it was hopeless, so hopeless that only Hort could have seriously envisaged it. But as a vision – as what the seventeenth century would call a 'Pisgah sight' – it foresaw a century of historical studies throughout the learned world. And if Hort himself never got nearer than the foothills, it was a great secular historian, W. M. Ramsay, who wrote at

Hort's death of the loss Ancient History had sustained in the passing of one whose 'work is a sure and strong foundation for the historian to work on ... as it could never have been had he not been guided by a wide outlook over the whole field of contemporary history'.

Ecclesiastical History, then, properly regarded as within a History Faculty, is also an integral part of the study of theology. Newman observed profoundly that if you drop any part of truth from the circle of knowledge

> you cannot keep its place vacant – the other sciences close up, or in other words they exceed their proper bounds and intrude where they have no right.

Take away church history, and into the vacuum there will come the history of ideas and the sociology of religion, but they will not fill the space, and they may soon get out of hand. To substitute for church history a programme of 'Religious Life and Thought' may be to proffer a subject whose back will break in half.

We may suppose that the indispensable quality of a historian is an imaginative scepticism, controlled by evidence. And it was the passion for accurate detail which was Hort's outstanding trait.

> He recognized [said Ryle] the importance of things that to less observant eyes seemed trifles : he never missed the right proportion of things : the tiny links were necessary to the chain : he never forgot the purpose of the chain in his work upon the links.

Armitage Robinson said that

> even more remarkable than the extent of his knowledge was his accuracy. He never seemed to trust to memory. Book after book came down from the shelves in the course of conversation : fact after fact was verified.[8]

For the historian, '1066' is as important as 'All That'. A recent writer discussing the theory of history mentioned that Luther appeared before the Diet of Worms in 1525, and since he repeated this wrong date four times on one page one could only suppose that, eminent historian though he was, he had either got this one wrong, or thought it too trivial to matter. Yet this cuts deep into the stuff of history : its irreversibility, the flow of time onwards and forwards. Germany in 1525 was vastly different from 1521 because of those earlier happenings, because of Luther, who he was and what he did. And also by reason of numbers of quite fortuitous happenings but for which we might now think of Martin of Wittenberg as another of those scholars like Henry Totting of Oyta or Perez of Valencia whom it is the latest one-upmanship to drag from well-deserved oblivion as the real clue-makers of the later Middle Ages.

History happens forwards but it is recorded and remembered and interpreted backwards – and this is the tension of the historian's craft and its high moments, those salmon leaps of imaginative perception. And here Hort's mastery of other disciplines is important. He brought to single words the loving attention which he gave to his Alpine flowers. His training in philosophy enabled him to spot fallacies and marshal evidence, and to suspect all hasty judgments. As a daisy by the river's brim held mysteries for him beyond the wisdom of Solomon to conceive, so for him a Biblical word was something which you might extract layer under layer of meaning – or like a jewel which might reflect one colour after another when held to the light – a splendid example of this is his exposition of 1 Peter 1 : 23–24. He had a sense of the unity of truth which looks back to the Christian scholars of the sixteenth century, to Ficino, Celtis and Vadianus, but which in its openness towards science looks forward to our own day. Dr Moulton said of it : 'much has been said of Dr Hort's versatility . . . but all those fields in which he delighted to roam were one', and he quoted Hort's own words in his luminous essay on Coleridge : 'there is no separation between the different subjects of his thoughts, still less between his thoughts, still less between his thoughts and life.'

Hort's few historical writings but partially reveal the depth of his learning. It was important for him that the New Testament itself is part of historical study and that it must be read within the history of the Early Church, and judged by the historical evidence. His canons of textual criticism in the famous introduction to the Westcott and Hort text are, as Professor Whitney said, principles which can be applied with but little adaptation to any field of historical criticism – to texts about the Roman Primacy in Irenaeus or Cyprian – or to the layers of Luther's *Table Talk* or the tangled manuscript problems of the first four chapters of his lectures on the Psalms. They are also a curiously up-to-date discussion of 'redaction criticism' for they examine the deep psychological impulses behind men's choice of words – and are equally relevant not only to the mind of the author of a gospel, but to the investigator of the visions of St Elisabeth of Schönau, of Henry VIII's love letters to Anne Boleyn, or Surgeon Beatty's account of the death of Nelson.

His score of encyclopaedia articles for the first volume of the *Dictionary of Christian Biography* – they never got beyond the A's and B's – are masterpieces which all who become entangled in this rather difficult and frustrating art form may study with profit. And they will be abashed by the accuracy, the care with which every possible and accessible authority has been weighed. He who reads the two great articles on the Gnostics Bardaisan and Basilides will find that Hort listens as patiently and one might almost say as reverently to their exotic jargon as though he were listening to the Apostles. And perhaps this is the high art of the historian, to sit down patiently before the evidence, to listen to it if it may be without preconceptions and forejudgment, until one hears undertones and undertones such as only a disciplined love of truth and, one might add, imaginative compassion can wring from the study of the past. I said he might be one of the last great amateurs, but perhaps somewhere in these two articles – more even than in Lightfoot's masterly article on 'Eusebius' – is the dividing line between the age of Macaulay and of Froude and that of modern historical-theological criticism.

His writings on Judaistic Christianity, on the Christian Ecclesia, and on the Clementine Literature, and the slighter essays on the Ante-Nicene Church were posthumously published and lack his finishing touches. The two B.D. and D.D. 'Dissertations' are small masterpieces about which there is nothing to add but a lament on the sad inflation of this good word 'Dissertation' which now appears to mean a longish essay, the dregs of a long vacation mingled with the scourings of two busy terms, jammed between lectures, supervisions, parties and great student argument. About Hort's involvement in a project to write a life of Simon de Montfort for boys one does not know whether to cheer or weep. Not even the need of a country parson to make ends meet, or a desire, as he said, to counter the Dickens and *Punch* depreciation of the past, can really excuse this diversion of his talents and time. But at least the publisher deserved what he got, which was a letter saying that the work was held up since Hort was reading all known chronicles on the subject, Pauli, Eccleston, Adam Marsh and Roger Wendover : and yet another, saying that there would need to be further delay, for he had heard of manuscripts in the British Museum and the Tower of London, and finally the concession that a book for boys need not have long footnotes, though of course all the references must be printed in full. The only result was a learned essay, 'The Last Days of Simon de Montfort', and the little boys had to make do with *Tom Brown's Schooldays* and *Westward Ho!*

No doubt here was a failure to concentrate interests and to express himself which marked a deep infirmity. He himself deplored the painful shyness which cut him off from his children. But it was more than shyness which kept him in those long small hours at Hitchin staring at blank paper for words which would not come, for sermons to parishioners who might have valued what he said as highly and understood him just as much, had he spoken to them off the cuff.

But it was not all infirmity either. There was the lavish generosity with which he gave time for his friends. He must have verified thousands of references for the edition of Marriott's *Remains* and Mackenzie's Hulsean Essay and he shortened his life by giving what remained of ebbing strength to pay tribute to Lightfoot.

And there were his pupils, about whom he took pains the long, hard way which anticipated what is known as 'non-directive teaching'. He would send a student away for weeks and, when he returned, comment : 'I thought you would come to see it; I am only surprised you did not see it sooner.'

> He would guide [said Armitage Robinson] where guidance was really needed : he would always sympathize and encourage . . . but on the other hand he seemed to regard the formation of an opinion as a very sacred thing : he refused to prejudice by arguing with one who was beginning to study a subject.

'What books would you recommend as the best introduction to the Synoptic problem?' After some sympathetic preface came the words never to be forgotten: 'I should advise you to take your Greek Testament and get your own view of the facts first of all.'

There was ill-health too, especially after his major breakdown in 1860–3. And some of it was a thoroughness which was the smiling despair of his colleagues, as when Westcott sent a manuscript to Mrs Hort asking her to produce it at teatime when he could only mark it with ticks and crosses, but asking her to snatch it from him at once and post it back if he showed the slightest signs of pursuing things further.

But most of all it was, as his son recognized, a crushing sense of responsibility. In an unpublished letter to W. M. Sanday, Hort defends his own

> unwillingness to accept a mere balancing of indecisive evidence when there is fair reason to hope that a little more work will bring sufficiently decisive evidence to light .

and he thinks it

> worthwhile to sacrifice much grudged time in order to make a trustworthy opinion possible

and comments that

> even the greatest of our German friends are for ever building on sandy foundations because they work too quickly to gather materials adequate for the confident judgements which exact no time.[9]

And here one cannot forbear a side glance at his young contemporary Adolf Harnack, also a noble spirit and a great scholar. In another letter to Sanday, Hort says of Harnack's *History of Dogma* that he is

> greatly taken by it.... I expected a really great book and I do not think I shall be disappointed.... But – some of the obiter dicta that have caught my eye ... do seem to me to be very rash and baseless indeed. His speed is to me a constant marvel, but it is a great snare to him. He seems never to have been taught to think three times before he speaks.[10]

To which Harnack might have retorted that it is hardly necessary to chew every word thirty-two times.

The contrasts are plain to see. Harnack had ninety writings out before he was twenty-seven, and at the height of his career produced 455 writings in fourteen years. And then, Berlin was not Cambridge. As Professor Harnack ambled amiably through the Tiergarten the Emperor might charge by with a loud hunting party, or Bismarck solidly stump along the allee, while in some by-path one might see Field Marshal von Moltke ruminating, hands clasped behind him, to whom a bow and a 'Good morning, Herr Generalfeldmarschall'[11] might be addressed and even elicit a jerky nod or a friendly glare. How different from the home life of St Peter's Terrace, or those Backs where eminences stroll indeed, but invariably *in statu pupillari*.

But on closer examination there are important similarities. It was not only Harnack who could spin theories. Armitage Robinson said of Hort that 'his mind was most astonishingly fertile in hypotheses'. It has been noticed that it is Hort, not Lightfoot, who went in for generalizations. And in that important letter to Lightfoot of 1 May 1860, which does I think reveal that Hort went beyond his colleagues in his openness to historical criticism, Hort could even add :

> I believe I am imprudent in sometimes uttering in conversation rude and premature conjectures and suspicions, which I have not had time to test and work out, and which persons of a more guarded temperament would probably under such circumstances keep to themselves.[12]

Both Harnack and Hort refused to drive a wedge between the New Testament and early church history. Both believed that it belongs to the historian to balance the wider perspective with the detail. 'It is always a danger', said Harnack, 'to lose the feeling for knowledge in its wider aspect when one is working among the details, but it is even worse to lose touch with those details.'[13] Both saw the history of the Early Church as the one pivotal, indispensable period of church history, not only because, as Professor Whitney said, it is the one period which the church historian can claim as specially his own, but because in it those fundamental questions are asked, if not answered, above which and towards which the whole of subsequent church history must forever spiral. For both of them it was all-important that doctrine should be studied in its historical context, and ideas examined at the point in history where they emerge.

> For the historian, [said Harnack] the most important period of all is the early Church – here are the measuring rods for all the rest, and if a historian has not been properly rooted in the study of this period he will go wrong in his judgements about what comes later. Because all the decisive questions in Church history are raised in this first period, so the Church historian needs to be at home here above all.

The two men never met, though it is pleasant to think that they might have met at the top of one of those lovely Alpine slopes which drew them both. Harnack once pointed to an Alpine hut and said, 'I would leave all this vision of beauty if I could go into that hut and find there a human being to whom I could talk.' It would be a pretty 'imaginary conversation' to picture Hort in that hut, staring out of the window, silent before the vast and entrancing spate of Harnack's words, finally dashing past him murmuring, 'Excuse me, but I think I can see the rare *Astragalus alopecuroides.*'

In his rather abortive Birkbeck Lectures, A. C. Headlam spoke of three schools of church history – of Lightfoot and Hort of England and Harnack of Germany and Mgr Duchesne of France. In his beautiful and moving essay, *Portrait de M. Pouget*, Jean Guitton has painted the picture of an old, blind, Catholic professor who might almost have been a Catholic Hort. 'It was Duchesne', says the old man, 'who opened the eyes of my spirit. I read Duchesne. I verified his texts : they were not many, but they were good. Then I read X – out of five references, three were wrong. I threw him away.'[14]

We may never knew how much Hort himself suffered the *Anfechtungen* of the nineteenth-century crisis of European conscience. But at Cambridge theology does not seem to have been, as at Oxford and London and Aberdeen and Berlin and Paris, a discipline 'under the Cross'. In England even the poignant clash of generations revealed in Gosse's *Father and Son* lacks something of the pathos of the tragic letter in which Mrs Harnack tried to assuage the deep wounds caused both to Father Theodosius, the great Lutheran dogmatist, and the son Adolf about some of whose writings his father could not bear to speak.

Or again, Hort would have agreed with the last words written by another Irishman, Fr George Tyrrell:

> Where the spirit is, there is liberty.... God has inaugurated a new epoch in man's intellectual life and extended his lordship over nature.... Shall he do less for man's spiritual life when the times are ripe, and are they not ripening?

But what must the Abbé Bremond have thought, who knew them both, if he compared the inspiring story of Hort's funeral in Cambridge with the dark tragedy of Tyrrell's burial at Storrington?

If Hort was born free into a tradition of unfettered enquiry from which others could only be liberated at cost, it was not that there was no price to pay, but that it had been paid already. For behind the Cambridge Victorians, the classical scholars, the scientists, the poets, the divines, there stand those Cambridge Platonists whose image confronted Hort daily in the Chapel of Emmanuel with their reminder that the spirit of man is the candle of the Lord, and the light of truth unquenchable. And behind them, the Cambridge Puritans – like him of Christ's, repudiating truth as a fugitive and cloistered virtue, or those others who like Hort himself were men of great learning well content to give a score of years and all they had of wisdom to the little people in small country parishes. And behind them too, the Cambridge Reformers who knew truth as that for which all men owe God a death.

Hort stands before us as the embodiment of that unfashionable ideal, the Man of Learning. But there was nothing in this of the pendant or the antiquarian, rather an eager stretching forward to what may lie ahead, which would welcome new truths, new disciplines. He believed that it was right and proper for students to turn to modern and to contemporary church history, since, as Newman said, new questions demand new answers. And yet he knew also that the lessons of the past may often be those which run counter to the spirit of the age.

It has been well said [he confessed] that it belongs to a University to be a refuge for unpopular doctrines, the storehouse where truths long said to have been exploded are preserved from oblivion until their hour comes round again. This is to claim for a University the high privilege of escaping subjection to each surging wave of opinion as it hides the ocean before it follows its predecessor out of sight . . . and of maintaining . . . that cause which finds fewest spokesmen in the world without.

Nor was Hort a dilettante, but rather an emblem of true academic freedom. Why should a man not turn from the rocks which speak of the first days of the world to the manuscripts which record the last days of Simon de Montfort, from the sacred text of Holy Scripture to the word of God not less truly written in the lilies of the field? If men may give their lives in pursuit of money, or ambition, or squander their gifts in endless trivialities, why should not this man spend his life in the pursuit of truth? It would not go down well, I dare say, with the University Grants Committee if our University were altogether composed of Horts. The credibility gap between Oxbridge and Plateglass and Moscow and Berkeley, California, is not likely to be bridged that way. But might it not in the long run be even more disastrous if we ceased to have room among us for such men of learning? And when we listen to a Robbins report with its painful confusion of learning and research, and its dreary vista of endless processions of eager beavers chasing an alphabetic jungle of slightly higher degrees, we want to say – 'Tell it not in Gath, rather tell the Department of Education and Science; whisper it not in the streets of Ashkelon, rather cry it aloud in the corridors of Westminster and Whitehall – that a University is a seat of Learning, and that in the long run wisdom is justified by her children.'

And we, who were taught by Hort's pupils, or by his pupils' pupils – who know something of that succession between teacher and taught, who have seen among our contemporaries, friends, teachers, colleagues, men after Hort's own heart, patient, honest seekers after a truth which never needs to strive or cry aloud – know that here is something not willingly to be let die.

To become disabled from unlearning [said Hort] is to have become disabled for learning. And when we cease to learn, we let go from us whatever of vivid knowledge we have hitherto possessed.

Westcott and Lightfoot go well in stained glass windows after the manner of the Western Church; Hort belongs to mosaic, to the great Eastern Doctors of whom he loved to speak. He might have made his last word to us what Ignatius of Antioch wrote when he reached forward to a martyr's crown:

νῦν γὰρ ἀρχὴν ἔχω τοῦ μαθητεύεσθαι, καὶ προσλαλῶ ὑμῖν ὡς συνδιδασκαλίταις μου.[15]

11

Gerard Manley Hopkins and the Theology of the Cross*

Superb ornamentation, magnificent work ...
There had never been such lovely things before him,
And no one else has ever put them on,
But only his own sons. *Ecclus.* 45 : 15 (*Jerusalem Bible*).

THE WRITER is describing the beautiful garments of Aaron the priest and the long line of his successors. Solomon in all his glory, he seems to say, was not arrayed like one of these. And yet among the people of God there is another priesthood of prophet, preacher, and poet, adorned with words. A priesthood after the order of Melchizedek, out of the blue, where each has to do his own thing :

There had never been such lovely things before him,
And no one else had ever put them on.

Yet his is a communicable vision — he makes others see what he has seen. He has his sons. When Canon Martin in his fine little book on Hopkins says :

I have ... received from these poems stimulus, light, and encouragement of inestimable spiritual value both in my prayers and daily living.[1]

he speaks for many of us, and he explains why we have come together here tonight.

One of the things which I trot out from time to time at school Speech Days is the well worn platitude : 'School is not just preparation for life. It is real life.' To an amazing and rather terrifying extent we go on being what we became at school. That was true of Gerard Manley Hopkins.

* The Third Annual Hopkins Sermon, preached at St Michael's Parish Church, Highgate, London, on Trinity Sunday, 6 June 1971, on the 127th Anniversary of the Birth of Gerard Manley Hopkins

It is true that part of his story reads like something out of *Tom Brown's Schooldays* or *Eric, or Little by Little* – the pale, thin youth reading his New Testament each night amid ridicule which dwindled into respect as they realized that he was, after all, no prig. And yet he had his own inscape. There was that passionate sense of justice which brought him into conflict with the Headmaster, the formidable Dr Dyne. Dr Dyne was an empire-builder, after the manner of another headmaster of whom it was said that he was 'a beast, but a just beast'. It was said of him by an old boy, 'His argument was always, 'Hold your tongue, sir!'', his conviction that boys must always be in the wrong, his appeal never to reason, always to force.' There is something to be said on his side. The boys who sat in this church a hundred years ago planned fights during the sermon and were rather modern in more than their hair-dos. 'Skin' Hopkins was a teen-age rebel. He could protest and demonstrate on behalf of sixth-form rights. But when for a bet he went without drink for three whole weeks until his tongue was black he hardly knew that what he had done was silly and dangerous, deserving reprimand. It all came to a climax in that terrible scene with Hopkins, as he said, 'wildly cheeking' a Headmaster lashing at him with a riding-whip. A traumatic experience? Certainly his 'thing' about injustice, his inability to see it without protest runs through all his life and into the most poignant of his later poems when he addresses God himself as though he were the Great Headmaster :

> Thou art indeed just, Lord, if I contend
> With thee; but, sir, so what I plead is just.

'But, sir . . .'

Hampstead and Highgate were full of artists, some in his own family. Here his love of nature, his talent for drawing, for music grew and matured. This week has seen the fourth centenary of Albrecht Dürer and we may wonder whether anybody has ever seen a violet as Dürer and Hopkins saw it, except God himself. Yet beneath the juice and the joy in leaf and tree there is the ground bass, the search for justice, for righteousness – the summons to renunciation. The Jesuits did not give him concern for renunciation. His concern for it made him a Jesuit, as John Henry Newman clearly saw.

There is the story of his holiday in Switzerland when he refused to let his Protestant Swiss guide shoulder his heavy pack, explaining the theological reason for bearing his own burden, to get the shocked and rather profound reply, 'Le Bon Dieu n'est comme ça' – God is good, he isn't like that.

Renunciation – decision – vocation : to become a Catholic, to become a priest, to become a Jesuit – to wound father and mother for Christ's sake, to become time's eunuch for the Kingdom of Heaven.

Nov. 6th, 1865. On this day by God's grace I resolved to give up all beauty until I had His leave for it.

The massacre of his innocents, the burning of his poems.

While he was at Highgate School there was for a few months a master, differing at all points from Dr Dyne, a shy, dreaming, kindly parson named R. W. Dixon. I have an interest in him, for his name was Richard Watson – after his grandfather, the first Methodist theologian after John Wesley, and his father, Dr Dixon, was a President of the Methodist Conference who taught in Richmond College where I once taught. So he grew up in the new Victorian Gothic building and he was confirmed in the Church of England as many Wesleyans still were. But when he went to Oxford he became a Tractarian and joined the Pre-Raphaelite Brotherhood, to become himself a divine, an artist and a poet. But this was not so much renunciation, as escape from the drab sub-culture of the Methodists. Perhaps as a result Dixon never became more than a beautiful and ineffectual angel. Hopkins, too, lived in that world of Liddon and Pusey, of Morris and Burne-Jones. Perhaps it was the drastic character of Hopkins's renunciation that saved his poetry as well as his soul. When he murdered his darlings, and followed the destruction of his poems with seven years elected silence, he cut himself off, as Dixon failed to do, from romanticism and from that dilettantism never far from the Pre-Raphaelite world. The result is that, after a century, Dixon's poems are dated, while it is Hopkins who fans fresh our wits with wonder. Dixon – his Methodist ancestry may have had something to do with it – was shaken to the core : like the Swiss guide he did not believe that God is like that. But Hopkins had a reply :

When a man has given himself to God's service, when he has denied himself and followed Christ, he has fitted himself to receive and does receive from God a special guidance, a more particular providence . . . if you value what I write, if I do myself, much more does our Lord.

Of course there was frustration, waste, suffering. We've all laughed at wartime farces about soldiers enlisting, and the expert cook is told to be an engineer and the engineer peels the potatoes. It happens in Christ's Church Militant from time to time, and it happened in that brigade of guards which was the Society of Jesus in Victorian days. Father Devlin speaks about Hopkins's three wounds, the frustration of his hopes to be a scholar, a preacher, a writer, but perhaps they were appropriately five wounds: the frustration of his spirit as a poet and an artist who needed above all liberty and, if not recognition, at least understanding.

And Hopkins, too, thought with the Church, which had not got round to *De Ecumenismo*. There is his sad comment on his beloved Henry Purcell 'listed to a heresy' for whom he seems to have felt that the only trumpets to sound on the other side must be the last Trump. And there is his comment, on which I must now speak, about St Gertrude and Martin Luther:

> Gertrude, lily, and Luther, are two of a town,
> Christ's lily and beast of the waste wood.

'Beast of the waste wood' – modern Catholic scholarship has moved far from this view of Luther. And yet this is perhaps the place to stress the ecumenical significance of Gerard Manley Hopkins to suggest that at their deepest level evangelical and Catholic Christianity are one. The Wreck of the Deutschland' is among other things a profound and moving exposition of the doctrine of Justification by Faith alone. Despite all its difficulties, the poem is from a theological point of view, a miracle of communication for it puts the whole view of salvation, in Paul, Augustine and Luther into a poem which entirely avoids the vocabulary of theology.

And when he cried out 'Where can I find a gracious God?' it is Hopkins and not John Osborne who explains Luther:

I did say yes
O at lightning and lashed rod;
Thou heardst me truer than tongue confess
Thy terror, O Christ, O God; ...
The frown of his face
Before me, the hurtle of hell
Behind, where, where was a, where was a place?

Luther found the place, the mercy seat. For centuries the two great words 'Justitia-justice' and 'Misericordia-mercy' had lain in theological text books, but side by side, unreconciled. Luther's greatest interpreter, Karl Holl, sees this as the breakthrough.

God does not send his grace alongside or past or instead of his justice : he sends it through his justice – God is nothing else than sheer self-giving goodness. This was more than a new exposition of Romans 1.17. It was the fountain of a new view of God.

Not new – perhaps, but as Catholic Josef Lortz says, 'new for Luther'. And so for Hopkins, mastery and mercy are one :

Lightning and love ...

This is the Catholic, this the evangelical experience :

Whether at once, as once at a crash Paul,
Or as Austin, a lingering-out swéet skíll.

Gertrude and Luther were indeed two of a town. In Luther's Thuringia, heart land of the Reformation, there flourished in the thirteenth century a company of holy women, Gertrude of Helfta, Gertrude of Hackeborn, Mechthild of Hackeborn, Mechthild of Magdeburg – out of whose prayers and pains (they were all chronic invalids) came a new pattern of spirituality, of devotion to the sacred humanity of Our Lord, and of his Five Wounds, a theology of the Cross. It was still there in the six-teenth century, in the poignant carvings in the churches where Luther grew up, and in the prayers of his teachers like John Staupitz. But as Hopkins joined his own anguished search for justice to the Exercises of Ignatius so Luther added to this theology of the Cross his need to understand the righteousness of

God. Luther and Hopkins make a duet. Luther, too, came to decision, 'walled around by agony and terror' – and looked back long after to

> That night, that year
> Of now done darkness I wretch lay wrestling with (my God!)
> my God.

Luther talked of his heart as an unsearchable abyss :

> O the mind, mind has mountains; cliffs of fall
> Frightful, sheer, no-man-fathomed. Hold them cheap
> May who ne'er hung there.

Both Luther and Hopkins drew the lesson of this for life, for vocation. We are to be Christ's to one another, says Luther – and Hopkins :

> . . . the just man justices;
> Keeps gráce : thát keeps all his goings graces;
> Acts in God's eye what in God's eye he is –
> Chríst. For Christ plays in ten thousand places.

If this were all we might leave them to the existentialists. But Luther's experience drew him to the midst of a great church struggle, to watch the shipwreck of an age. He hit the headlines. And so Hopkins, too, in the second part of his great poem turns us to our newspapers.

That part of the Kentish sandbanks with their wrecks is news for us, though we think rather of the inconvenience of oil slicks than of loss of life. For us an air crash with its stereotyped pattern of horror is what shipwrecks were a hundred years ago. I have a newspaper cutting of 1882, describing a wreck off New York of the *City of Colombus* – with the same pattern as the wreck of the *Deutschland*, the long torment of the elements, the cruel irony of sight of land, the vain gestures of heroism, the passengers climbing the rigging to fall off one by one. Here is the real world but Hopkins bids us look not at it but through it to the ultimate 'Why' of natural disaster and human suffering.

Hopkins whose month, like Mary's, was May, for whom blue skies were almost a beloved obsession, draws the blackness of a

December night : he who could spend pages describing the lovely breaking of a wave, or the shape of a single snowflake, shows us what terrors these can become when God's creation gets out of hand in hurricane and blizzard.

There is one difference between the holiday steamer *City of Columbus* and the immigrant steamer, the *Deutschland* – that circle of five nuns, dying hand in hand, and their tall leader crying 'O Christ, Christ, come quickly!' Here is a third dimension. The world within us, the world without us. And over them both *'Ipse*, the only one, Christ, King, Head'. Karl Barth says that a friend is one who, at the end of the day, is for us. You might say that Hopkins has nothing to say about suffering which Job had not said long before, only that for Jahweh he substitutes the face of Christ. But is not that everything? Christ 'for us' as the great strokes of the Creed affirm : born, made man 'for us', dying 'for our sins', rising 'for our justification', who ever liveth to make intercession 'for us'. But if He be 'for us', who can be against us? So on this Trinity Sunday we confess One God, who is mastery and mercy.

The reader's attention is drawn to an error in the placing of the notes below. The following is the correct arrangement: Notes under Ch.2 refer to **Ch.4** (More and Tyndale); under Ch.4 refer to **Ch.6** (Parker); under Ch.5 refer to **Ch.7** (Bedell); under Ch.6 refer to **Ch.8** (Wesley); under Ch.7 refer to **Ch.9** (Newman); under Ch.8 refer to **Ch.10** (Hort); the note under Ch.9 refers to **Ch.11** (Hopkins); notes under Ch.10 refer to **Ch.3** (Luther).

Notes

Chapter 1

1 Quotations from the Rule are taken from Justin McCann (ed.), *The Rule of Saint Benedict in Latin and English* (London 1952)
2 Denys Hay, *Europe: the Emergence of an Idea* (Edinburgh 1968), pp. 83–4 quoted ibid., p. 110

Chapter 2

1 *Humanism and Poetry in the Early Tudor Period* (London 1959)
2 G. R. Elton, *Studies in Tudor and Stuart Politics and Government* (Cambridge 1974), i, 170–2
3 See the fine biography: Michael Balfour and Julian Frisby, *Helmuth von Moltke: a Leader against Hitler* (London 1972)
4 *Letter to the Duke of Norfolk* (London 1875), pp. 57, 66
5 ed. E. E. Reynolds (London 1963)

Chapter 4

1 *Correspondence of Matthew Parker, D.D., Archbishop of Canterbury*, ed. J. Bruce and T. T. Perowne (Parker Society 1853), p. 10
2 ibid., p. 11
3 ibid., p. 13
4 J. Strype, *Life and Acts of Matthew Parker* (London 1711), i, 45–6
5 *De Antiquitate Britannicae Ecclesiae* (1572)
6 *Correspondence*, p. 24
7 ibid., p. 28
8 ibid., p. x
9 ibid., p. viii
10 ibid., p. 59
11 ibid., p. 479
12 ibid., pp. 50–1; he had been appointed Dean of Lincoln in 1552
13 ibid., p. 57
14 ibid., p. x
15 ibid., p. 71
16 ibid., pp. 156–7
17 ibid., p. 158
18 ibid., p. 311
19 ibid., pp. 214–16
20 ibid., p. 147
21 ibid., pp. 188–9
22 ibid., pp. 478; this was his last letter to Cecil
23 ibid., p. 426; see also p. 434
24 ibid., p. 173: 'I think divers of my brethren will rather note me, if they were asked, too sharp and too earnest in moderation, which

towards them I have used, and will still do, till mediocrity shall be received amongst us' (Apri 1563)

25 ibid., p. 246
26 ibid., p. 268
27 ibid., pp. 277–9; see aso p. 237 : 'I alone they say am in fault . . . I only am the stirrer and the incenser'; also p. 263
28 ibid., pp. 280–1
29 ibid., p. 284
30 ibid., p. 364
31 L. Richmond, *The Fathers of the English Church* (London 1812), viii, 148–9
32 E. C. Hoskyns, *Cambridge Sermons*, ed. Charles Smyth (London 1938; paperback edn 1970); V : 'The Importance of the Parker Manuscripts in the College Library'
33 Yet Parker's *De Antiquitate Britannicae Ecclesiae* was privately printed, only a handful of copies being made. A sad footnote to a letter in 1574/5 (*Correspondence*, p. 474) says : 'I toy out my time, partly with copying of books, partly in devising ordinances for scholars to help the ministry, partly in genealogies, and so forth.' Parker himself never essayed the apologia
34 *Correspondence*, p. 479
35 ibid., p. 479
36 ibid., p. 176

Chapter 5
1 Pronounced 'Beedle'. His biographies are : (1) E. S. Shuckburgh (ed.), *Two Biographies of William Beedle, Bishop of Kilmore* (Cambridge 1902); (2) *A True Relation of the Life and Death of . . . William Bedell, Lord Bishop of Kilmore in Ireland*. Edited by Thomas Wharton Jones. Camden Society. New Series, IV (London 1872)
2 C. E. Raven, *John Ray, Naturalist* (Cambridge 1942), p. 2
3 See P. Collinson, *The Elizabethan Puritan Movement* (London 1967), p. 210
4 Shuckburgh, op. cit., p. 217
5 ibid., p. 223
6 *A Protestant Memorial or the Shepherd's Tale of the Pouder-Plott. A Poem in Spenser's Style* (London 1713)
7 Walton, *Lives* (Oxford 1968), p. 136
8 Joseph Hall, *Works* (1808), vii, 137–8
9 Smith, *The Life and Letters of Sir Henry Wotton* (Oxford 1907), i, 42
10 ibid., i, 58–71
11 Shuckburgh, op. cit., p. 225
12 Smith, op. cit., i, 90
13 ibid., i, 103
14 He also translated a tract by the renegade Archbishop of Spalato who came later to England but eventually reverted to Rome
15 (California 1968), Chapter 10
16 F. R. Bolton, *The Caroline Tradition of the Church of Ireland* (London 1958), p. 134
17 Shuckburgh, op. cit., p. 266
18 R. Buick Knox, *James Ussher, Archibshop of Armagh* (Cardiff 1967), p. 82

19 Ussher, *Works*, ed. Elrington (1847), i, 87
20 ibid., i. 88; here it is stated that a diary of William Bedell is preserved in the first Registry book of Trinity College
21 Knox, op. cit., p. 86
22 Edmund Spenser, *A View of the Present State of Ireland*, ed. W. L. Renwick (Oxford 1970)
23 Shuckburgh, op. cit., p. 312
24 ibid.
25 Ussher, *Works*, ed. cit., xv, 459
26 ibid., xv, 507
27 Lambeth MS. cod. 595
28 G. H. Turnbull, *Hartlib, Dury and Comenius* (Liverpool 1947), p. 14, n. 5
29 Shuckburgh, op. cit., p. 358
30 *The Copies of certain letters ... between Mr. James Waddesworth ... and W. Bedell* (London 1865)
31 Walton, *Lives*, p. 137
32 Shuckburgh, op. cit., p. 258

Chapter 6
1 'Anglican' is a nineteenth-century term and to a surprising extent conditions discussion in terms of hindsight, in terms of nineteenth-century parties: Anglo-Catholic, Evangelical and Broad Church. The result is such a biased and one-sided, if splendid, anthology as that of P. E. More and F. L. Cross's *Anglicanism*, and some descriptions of an Anglican *via media* which make very disputable reading of the seventeenth century, not least in the case of Richard Hooker, who in no way dominated Church of England divinity in the seventeenth and eighteenth centuries
2 Sermon 'On Zeal', in John Wesley, *Works*, ed. T. Jackson (London 1872), vii, 57
3 ibid., vii, 64
4 I find the eighteenth-century phrase 'inward religion' best to use. The word 'spirituality' has Catholic undertones, and the phrase fits the catholicity of Wesley's *Christian Library* and solves, as much as anything can, the question of the relation of mysticism to devotion
5 Doubtless in John Worthington's edition of 1677, from which John Wesley probably drew the title 'The Christian Pattern' for his own editions
6 Reprinted as an appendix in T. Jackson, *The Life of the Rev. Charles Wesley* (London 1841), ii, 500–34
7 ibid., ii, 510
8 ibid., ii, 521–2
9 ibid., ii, 524–5
10 *Works*, x, 480–500
11 ibid., x, 483
12 ibid., x, 483, 491–2
13 *The Letters of the Rev. John Wesley*, ed. John Telford (London 1931), v, 110
14 *Journal*, ed. Curnock, iii, 391 : 23 March 1749
15 ibid., vii, 352–3 : 15–18 January 1788
16 'A Compendium of Logic', in *Works*, xiv, 189

17 G. E. M. Anscombe, *Introduction to Wittgenstein's Tractatus*, 4th edn (London 1971), p. 172
18 Preface to *Sermons on Several Occasions* (1778); in *Works*, vi, 186–7
19 *Journal*, ed. Curnock, v, 169 : 5 June 1766
20 Sermon, 'The Wisdom of God's Counsels', in *Works*, vi, 328
21 *Journal*, ed. Curnock, iv, 354 : 20 September 1759
22 Sykes, *Church and State in England in the XVIIIth Century* (London 1934), pp. 398–9
23 Sermon, 'The Case of Reason Impartially Considered', in *Works*, vi, 359–60
24 Alexander Knox, 'Remarks on the Life and Character of John Wesley', in Robert Southey, *Life of Wesley and the Rise and Progress of Methodism*, ed. Maurice H. Fitzgerald (London 1925), ii, 352–3, 357
25 'Minutes of the Conference, 1744–45', in *Publications of the Wesley Historical Society*, No. 1 (London 1896), pp. 10, 22
26 *Letters*, ed. Telford, iv, 122
27 Knox, 'Remarks', in Southey, op. cit., ii, 345
28 Wesley, *Christian Library* (London 1820), ix, 376–7
29 ibid., ix, 378–9
30 Sermon, 'The Case of Reason Impartially Considered', in *Works*, vi, 359
31 F. A. Yates, *Giordano Bruno and the Hermetic Tradition* (London 1964); *The Rosicrucian Enlightenment* (London 1972); Daniel P. Walker, *The Ancient Theology: Studies in Christian Platonism from the 15th to the 18th Century* (London 1972); Charles E. Trinkaus, *In Our Image and Likeness: Humanity and Divinity in Italian Humanist Thought*, 2 vols (London 1970)
32 Heinrich Bornkamm, *Das Jahrhundert der Reformation: Gestalten und Kräfte* (Göttingen 1966), pp. 315–31, 331–45; Serge Hutin, *Les disciples anglias de Jacob Boehme aux xviie et xviiie siècles* (Paris 1960); P. Hutin, *Jacob Behmen et son influence sur les écrivains anglais du xvii siècle* (Paris 1964); Alexander Koyré, *Mystiques, spirituels, alchimistes: Schwenckfeld, Seb, Franck, Wiegel, Paracelse* (Paris 1955)
33 'Jakob Böhme : Leben und Wirkung', 'Jakob Böhme, der Denker'
34 On William Law and John Wesley, see John Brazier Green, *John Wesley and William Law* (London 1945); Eric W. Baker, *A Herald of the Evangelical Revival: a Critical Inquiry into the Relation of William Law to John Wesley and the Beginnings of Methodism* (London 1948); A. Keith Walker, *William Law: His Life and Thought* (London 1973)
35 For Wesley's comments on Böhme, see his 'Thoughts upon Jacob Behmen, 1780', in *Works*, ix, 509–18; *Journal*, ed. Curnock, iv, 409; iii, 17: 'Here I met once more with the works of a celebrated author, of whom many great men cannot speak without rapture and the strongest expressions of admiration – I mean Jacob Behmen . . . what can I say . . . ? . . . it is most sublime nonsense, inimitable bombast, fustian not to be paralleled !' See also John Byrom, *Private Journal and Literary Remains*, ed. R. Parkinson, Chetham Society, *Remains, etc.* vol. 2, part 2 (Manchester 1857), for the statement that Wesley read out a group of Behmenist and William Law addicts from his society.
36 Gordon Rupp, *Methodism in Relation to Protestant Tradition* (London 1954), p. 20; the 'optimism of grace', as I use the term, must be distinguished from the optimism of the Enlightenment; according to Peter

Gay, the word appears in the mid-eighteenth century – just in time to be shattered by the Lisbon earthquake!

37 Scougal, 'Discourses on Important Subjects', in *The Life of God in the Soul of Man* (London 1726), p. 247
38 'Remarks', in Southey, op. cit., ii, 344
39 'Minutes of the Conference, 14 May 1746', in *Minutes of the Methodist Conferences from the First Held in London by the late Rev. John Wesley in the Year 1744* (London 1862), i, 32
40 Alexander Knox, 'Remarks', in Southey, op. cit., ii, 353
41 Sermon, 'On God's Vineyard' (1787), in *Works*, vii, 206–7
42 Sermon, 'National Sins and Miseries' (1775), in *Works*, vii, 402
43 W. F. Lofthouse, 'Wesley and his Women Correspondents', in *Wesley's Chapel Magazine*, January 1959, pp. 2–8; April 1959, pp. 6–12
44 Alexander Knox, 'Remarks', in Southey, op. cit., ii, 339
45 *Journal*, ed. Curnock, vi, 209 : 1 September 1778
46 ibid., viii, 3 : 18 August 1789

Chapter 7
1 Alexander Whyte, *Newman: an Appreciation* (Edinburgh 1901), p. 11
2 W. G. Ward, *Life of Cardinal Newman* (London 1912), ii, 358–9
3 *Oxford High Anglicanism* (London 1895), pp. 31–2
4 ibid., p. 109
5 ibid., p. 132
6 ibid., p. 155
7 ibid., pp. 157–8; he has already noted that Newman 'was also a diligent novel reader'.
8 For a more critical estimate of Newman, see Lidgett's John Wesley and John Newman', in *God, Christ, and the Church* (London 1908)
9 Whyte, op. cit., p. 125
10 ibid., pp. 126–7
11 W. B. Selbie, *The Life of Andrew Martin Fairbairn* (London 1914), pp. 203 ff.
12 ibid., p. 206; Ward, op. cit., ii, 505 ff.
13 Privately printed 1890; pp. 69 ff.
14 W. B. Selbie, op. cit., p. 208
15 G. F. Barbour, *The Life of Alexander Whyte D.D.* (London 1923)
16 Whyte, op. cit., pp. 65–6
17 G. F. Barbour, op. cit., pp. 194–5
18 ibid., p. 241
19 ibid., pp. 241–6
20 ibid., p. 290
21 ibid., p. 294
22 ibid., p. 295
23 ibid., p. 194
24 Whyte, op. cit., pp. 90–2
25 ibid., pp. 97–9
26 ibid., pp. 66–7
27 John Keble, quoted by Whyte, op. cit., p. 31
28 ed. Erich Przywára (London 1963)
29 Newman, *Letter to the Duke of Norfolk* (London 1875), p. 57
30 Whyte, op. cit., p. 118

31 *Apologia* (1881), p. 4
32 J. Calvin, *The Institutes of the Christian Religion*, trans. Thomas Norton (1561), I, i
33 ibid.
34 *Grammar of Assent;* see *The Heart of Newman*, ed. Przywára (London 1963), p. 11
35 *Apologia* (1881), p. 195

Chapter 8
1 The Rev. Professor W. O. Chadwick, D.D., Master of Selwyn College
2 J. P. Whitney, *The Study of Ecclesiastical History To-day* (Cambridge 1919), p. 10
3 S. Neill, *The Interpretation of the New Testament, 1861–1961* (London 1964)
4 A. F. Hort (ed.), *Life and Letters of Fenton John Anthony Hort*, 2 vols (London 1896)
5 H. E. Ryle, *Cambridge Review*, 8 December 1892
6 *Life and Letters*, ii, 424
7 ibid., i, 233–4
8 'The Late Professor Hort', in *Expositor*, 4th series, vii (1893), 64
9 Bodleian MS. Eng. misc. d. 140: 28 August 1889
10 ibid.: 27 February 1886
11 Agnes von Zahn-Harnack, *Adolf von Harnack* (Berlin 1951), pp. 131–2
12 *Life and Letters*, i, 420–1
13 Harnack to Holl, 1895, in K. Holl, *Briefwechsel mit Adolf von Harnack*, ed. Karpp (1966), p. 14
14 J. Guitton, *Œuvres Complètes*: I, *Portrait de M. Pouget* (Paris 1968)
15 *To the Ephesians*, 3, 1

Chapter 9
1 Philip M. Martin, *Mastery and Mercy: A Study of Two Religious Poems* (London 1957), p. xi

Chapter 10
1 *Young Man Luther: A Study in Psychoanalysis and History* (London 1959)
2 John Osborne, *Luther* (London 1961), p. 86
3 W. von Loewenich, 'Zein Jahre Lutherforschung in Deutschland', in *Von Augustin zu Luther* (1959), pp. 307 ff.; G. Müller, 'Neuere Literatur zur Theologie des jungen Luther', in *Kerygma und Dogma* (1965), pp. 325 ff. These essays are mainly concerned with Germany
4 *D. Martin Luthers Werke* (Weimar edn), 55
5 H. Bornkamm, 'Zur Frage der iustitia Dei beim Jungen Luther', in *Archiv für Reformationsgeschichte* (1962), ii, 11, n. 54
6 *Luthers Werke* (Weimar edn), xliv, p. 704, line 15
7 A. G. Dickens, *Reformation and Society in Sixteenth-Century Europe* (London 1966), p. 55
8 *Luther's Works*, ed. Lehmann (Philadelphia, Pa.), xxxvi, 228: 'Nichts ist so klein, Gott ist noch kleiner. Nichts ist so gros, Gott ist noch grösser. Nichts ist so kurtz, Gott ist noch Kürtzer. Nichts ist so lang, Gott ist noch lenger. Nichts ist so breit, Gott ist noch breiter. Nichts ist so schmal, Gott ist noch schmaler, and so fort an. Ists ein unausssprechlich wesen...; *Luthers Werke* (Weimar edn), xxvi, 339,39n–340,1
9 *Luthers Werke* (Weimar edn), Tr. 1, Nr 1160

Notes

Chapter 11

1 *St Francis of Assisi: 1226–1926: Essays in Commemoration* (London 1926), p. vi
2 J. H. Newman, *Lectures on the Present Position of Catholics in England*: addressed to the Brothers of the Oratory (London 1851), pp. 83–4
3 Rosalind B. Brooke (ed. & trans.), *Scripta Leonis, Rufini et Angeli Sociorum S. Francesci: The Writings of Leo, Rufino and Angelo Companions of St Francis* [Oxford Medieval Texts] (Oxford 1970), p. 235
4 *Scripta Leonis*, p. 9
5 F. C. Burkitt, 'St Francis of Assisi and some of his biographers', in *Franciscan Essays II* (Manchester 1932), p. 38
6 *Scripta Leonis*, pp. 126–33, 164–7
7 ibid., p. 131
8 L. T. Topsfield, *Troubadours and Love* (Cambridge 1975), p. 105
9 *Scripta Leonis*, p. 89
10 ibid., p. 95
11 ibid., p. 127
12 ibid., p. 175
13 ibid., p. 241
14 John Moorman, *A History of the Franciscan Order from its Origins to the Year 1517* (Oxford 1968), p. 35
15 Father Cuthbert, O.S.F.C., 'St Francis and Poverty', in Paul Sabatier *et al.*, *Franciscan Essays I* (Aberdeen 1912), p. 25
16 David Knowles, *Saints and Scholars: twenty-five medieval portraits* (Cambridge 1962), p. 92
17 Jean Guitton, *Œuvres Complètes: Critique Religieuse* (Paris 1968), p. 1213
18 Christopher Brooke, *Medieval Church and Society: Collected Essays* (London 1971). 'Paul Sabatier and St Francis of Assisi', p. 205
19 *Scripta Leonis*, pp. 14, 19
20 G. K. Chesterton, *St Francis of Assisi* (London 1923), p. 99
21 E. A. Armstrong, *St Francis, Nature Mystic* (London 1973)
22 Horace Waller (ed.), *The Last Journals of David Livingstone, in Central Africa, from 1865 to his death* (London 1874), ii, 42
23 F. C. Burkitt, 'The Study of the Sources of the Life of St Francis', in *St Francis of Assisi: 1226–1926*, p. 60
24 Leo Sherley-Price, *S. Francis of Assisi: His Life and Writings as recorded by his contemporaries* (London 1959), p. 166; E. A. Armstrong, op. cit., p. 146
25 John Moorman, op. cit., p. 55; citing *Mirror of Perfection*, 41
26 *Scripta Leonis*, pp. 60, 287
27 F. C. Burkitt, 'Fonte Colombo and its traditions', in *Franciscan Essays II*, p. 50
28 *Scripta Leonis*, p. 215
29 A. G. Ferrers Howell (trans.), *The Lives of S. Francis of Assisi by Brother Thomas of Celano* (London 1908), pp. 334–5
30 Quoted in Moorman, op. cit., p. 24
31 *Scripta Leonis*, p. 297